Praise for *The Little Book of Dyslexia*

Any parent of a child diagnosed with dyslexia would find this book excellent in that it is written by someone who really knows how that impacts. I love the human touch in Joe's style of writing. Would I buy this as a parent of a dyslexic person? Absolutely!

Andrew Massey, Fox In The Box Consulting Ltd

The Little Book of Dyslexia is easily accessible, written in an almost informal and 'chatty' way which makes the reader want to read on. The mix of fact and anecdote is timely and appropriate. The 'human' element of the book is its strongest selling point – the author knows what it is like to be dyslexic and how it impacts on everyday life and the use of humour (often at the author's expense!) is very apt, especially when describing situations/faux pas that can easily be made.

The book will appeal to trainee teachers, newly qualified teachers and practitioners across all phases of education. It will also prove to be a practical guide for all parents on how to cope with a child who has dyslexia, and also some reassurance that a 'diagnosis' of dyslexia is not life-inhibiting.

Debbie Coslett, Chief Executive Officer,
The Hayesbrook School Academy Trust

This may be a 'little book' but it is about a big subject and has great heart and a penetrating mind. It is a very useful book that is as much about the whole issue of learning as it is about dyslexia.

Joe Beech combines his personal story, a succinct account of the theory and research associated with dyslexia and a significant degree of practical recommendations that cannot fail to be of immense use to everyone who has experience of dyslexia – as subject, parent or teacher.

The way Joe tells his own story endears him to his readers and commands human attention to this most human of challenges – both in terms of learning in our social and educational systems and in terms of how we should regard a specific group of learners, numbering over two million people in this country alone. He charts his own experience from early childhood through to his expereinces in higher education – a story of obstacles surmounted and how those obstacles could and should be significantly reduced by those who manage learning systems.

The first five chapters introduce the reader to the subject itself, explaining the potential genetic origins of dyslexia and the questions it raises about the way that we think about learning and some of the many obstacles there are to learning within our social and educational systems. The three chapters dealing with the period of early years through to secondary school help us to get inside the mind of a child experiencing dyslexia and the typical response of the system to such a child. The 'system' includes teachers and parents in particular, for it is the personal response of the adults whom the child encounters that can profoundly influence whether learning for a child experiencing dyslexia becomes a pathway among many possible pathways, or a steep incline with ever-growing obstacles to be cleared in an increasingly isolating climate.

Joe charts the story with a light touch in which he offers us insights laced with humour and occasional irony as he helps us to understand how this particular challenge to learning can be effectively managed. His inference that we need to know our ACBs (deliberately a little ironic) – Assessment, Classroom practice and Behaviour – so that adults, particularly teachers and parents, can help move the learning of children with dyslexia forward and themselves develop a useful and practical level of understanding, has a powerful impact on the reader. He demystifies the subject, making it immediately accessible to anyone who wants to understand it and respond to it.

In spite of the plain and very accessible writing on the subject and its intensely practical nature, this is a book founded on thorough and rigorous research, From the earliest chapter he finds simple ways of explaining and illustrating what the printed environment might look like through dyslexic eyes, even with a spell-checker on the computer to hand (or eye).

The illustrations are particularly evocative and somehow create a feeling of empathy towards the person, young or more mature, working out how to manage this distinctive set of challenges.

One very serious point about this book is that it explores aspects of learning in general. What is written about dyslexia is applicable to all aspects of what we have come to call 'special needs'; and what we can learn from thinking about meeting special needs applies to the whole potenitally vexed question of how all of us learn. To read this book is to further deepen one's understanding of learning. To understand dyslexia and how to manage it is to grasp more about the management of learning for all children and indeed all adults. That is perhaps the most remarkable thing about this 'little' yet very big book.

Or perhaps there is one other thing that is most remarkable. It is that it is an example of *amor vincit omnia*. Joe's story is one of being loved and of loving – the key ingredients of how he has come thus far in his life managing challenges that are that bit steeper than those which we normally face. It is clear that this is due in no small part to the love he has experienced especially from his family. Equally he approaches the subject in a loving way – love for those like him who have engaged with this particular challenge, love of learning, love that he shows through the insights he shares in the book, and the love which has drawn him to a career in education himself – something he hints that many people find remarkable.

This is a 'must-read' not only for anyone who has met dyslexia – in their own approach to learning or in a child or childern they know – but for anyone who has an interest in learning and how it is best facilitated, whoever the learner might be. If you are interested in learning and being a more effective learner on a personal level, read this book.

Roger Pask, education leadership and management
consultant, facilitator and coach

Joe Beech is going to be an outstanding teacher. He is currently at the University of Chichester studying to be a PE teacher in secondary school. He is also the author of *The Little Book of Dyslexia*. This book is a very welcome addition to the library of books on dyslexia because it offers a personal account allied to a teacher's perspective. Even in these relatively enlightened days, not many people are both dyslexic and a teacher.

Joe Beech grew up in Kent where the 11 plus was still in operation so while his brother went off to grammar school, he went to a mixed high school. This had some key advantages. The school taught touch typing, which Joe acknowledges as 'one of the most valuable skills' that he possesses. While so many books focus on endless spelling and phonics practice, *The Little Book of Dyslexia* is a breath of fresh air when it comes to the practical uses of technology to support the dyslexic learner. Beech talks about mind mapping, dictaphones, e-readers, smartphones and all the panoply of 'technology in your back pocket'.

Joe Beech's experiences have informed his approach to his new career. It is worth buying this book for the chapter on teaching alone. There is a wealth of practical tips: Do a lesson plan as a flow chart instead of in the conventional way so you can see exactly where you are and where you are going.

'The best resource available to you in any classroom is the pupils themselves,' says Joe. 'If you can implement a system in which the pupils cover most of the organisation, half of the work is done for you!' He suggests building on the ideas used in *The Apprentice* and setting up a system where pupils take on roles as Project Manager, Resource Manager, Team Motivator, the

Accountant who is responsible for rewards and the Coach/ Mentor who also acts as assessor. Not only does this motivate young people but it also prepares them for the world of work, too.

Joe Beech has produced a very enjoyable read which offers an insight into the best teaching too: 'The best lectures and lessons I have had are the ones that caught me off-guard and involved a novel experience which remained in my mind.' I am sure his own lessons will be equally memorable.

Sal McKeown, freelance journalist and author of *How to help your Dyslexic and Dyspraxic Child* (Crimson Publishing)

This little book is a delightful read. Written by a trainee PE teacher who was diagnosed at the age of 8 with dyslexia and dyspraxia, it is a testament to his perseverance through a sometimes unforgiving education system bent on teaching literacy and numeracy in dyslexia-unfriendly ways. Aimed primarily at teachers, *The Little Book of Dyslexia* has a wealth of practical information to help both teachers and parents meet the needs of dyslexic children more effectively.

There is a good balance between the author's own experience, tools of the trade and literature research all adding up to well-rounded package addressing the needs of dyslexic pupils and students in education. Explaining how dyslexia is experienced is helpful as it puts the reader in the shoes of dyslexic pupils focusing on issues such as self-esteem, organisational skills and managing challenging behaviour and how these impact on learning.

The book also has suggestions about useful software to support dyslexic students and ideas for teachers to consider in their classroom practice. The section on exams is particularly useful. The author takes a balanced view about exams versus coursework and suggests a number of strategies to help dyslexic students through these challenging times. Topics such as managing time and money are covered as well as organisational skills. These are essential life skills for all young adults. The last section of the book is specifically aimed at teachers, packed with ideas about how to make classrooms dyslexia-friendly.

The Little Book of Dyslexia is a gem of a book that will be useful for working with all pupils and students. It is packed with common sense strategies and insights that will make learning fun and productive.

Carol Frankl, Ofsted Inspector
and a provider of SEN training and consultancy

THE LITTLE BOOK OF
DYSLEXIA

Both sides of the classroom

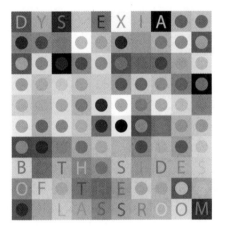

Joe Beech
Edited by Ian Gilbert

Independent Thinking Press

First published by
Independent Thinking Press
Crown Buildings, Bancyfelin, Carmarthen, Wales, SA33 5ND, UK
www.independentthinkingpress.com

Independent Thinking Press is an imprint of Crown House Publishing Ltd.

First published 2013.

British Library Cataloguing-in-Publication Data
A catalogue entry for this book is available
from the British Library.

Print ISBN 978-1-78135-010-2
Mobi ISBN 978-1-78135-015-7
ePub ISBN 978-1-78135-016-4

Printed and bound in the UK by
Gomer Press, Llandysul, Ceredigion

I would like to dedicate this book to my better half, my family and friends without whom I would not have achieved a lot of the things that I have today, this book included. In particular I would like to thank my parents for all their support whilst I was growing up and my mother for inspiring me into the world of education and teaching, although I get a strange look sometimes when I tell people that.

I would also like to extend particular thanks to my new fiancée Sarah, for all of her love, patience and support. I will love you always.

One day I may find a way to put my love into words but until then I will dedicate a book to you which is about how hard it is to put things into words.

Much love.

Contents

Acknowledgements

I would like to sincerely acknowledge all of the hard work and support that has gone into making this book a reality. First and foremost I would like to extend huge thanks to Ian Gilbert for providing me with this fantastic opportunity and giving me fantastic support along the way. I would also like to thank everyone at Independent Thinking Press for their fantastic work, support and patience.

I would like to thank my wonderful Grandma, Rose Soper, for providing me with these wonderful illustrations which bring a bit of life to my words. Thanks for your great work and creativity.

I would also like to extend thanks to my mother Carrie for sharing her astonishing knowledge of the education system and list of rather useful contacts which is an endless help. On top of that she continues to be one of the many people who have proofread my work.

I would also like to thank some of those contacts including Janet Kane from Hayesbrook School for Boys for providing some very useful real world examples of working with children with dyslexia. Both Andy Vass and Roger Pask also deserve mention for providing some inspirational courses which I occasionally draw from.

Last, but by no means least, I would like to extend thanks to all of my sources and reference authors in particular the British Dyslexia Association for their wonderful work and as a particularly good starting point for anyone interested in dyslexia.

If I have missed anyone then please feel free to berate me upon which I will proceed to attempt to shower you with praise!

Foreword

Asking someone with dyslexia to write a book might be seen as a cruel joke. Like inviting a vegetarian with a fear of clowns to go to McDonalds. But who better to write a book for teachers about a condition that affects so many young people than someone who has first-hand experience of school life with dyslexia?

If you are a teacher, then you will be teaching children with dyslexia, whether you 'believe' in the condition or not. (Yes, there are some out there who still see it as an affliction made up by bad spellers.) Whether you are able to spot them or not is a different matter. In fact, your ability to spot them is down to your knowledge of what dyslexia really entails. After reading this fascinating and enlightening book I guarantee there will be several children in your classes whom you will look at with fresh eyes.

So, before you start, lets get some things straight. Whilst the word 'dyslexia' means literally 'difficulty with words' – and is a word interestingly that has only been around since the 1960s – dyslexia is about much more than spelling. In fact, like Robin Williams in *Happy Feet 2,* difficulty spelling is just an annoying little tip on a very big iceberg. The child with dyslexia is likely to have a wider range of challenges than dealing with words and, in many cases, spelling is the least of their battles.

Take, for example, the idea of 'executive functioning'. This is the process by which our brains work to ensure we are doing the right things in the right ways to achieve whatever it is that we are trying to achieve. It's like the conductor in an orchestra, silently guiding the whole to ensure that that whole is greater than the sum of its parts. Within the remit of executive functioning are instruments such as working memory, planning, attention, problem solving, verbal reasoning, inhibition, our capacity for blocking out distractions not related to the task and our ability to switch quickly to plan B when plan a isn't working. Unfortunately, according to research reported in *Dyslexia – an International Journal of Research and Practice,** 'children with dyslexia demonstrate impairments in a variety of executive functions'. In other words, the child with dyslexia is going through a whole series of battles and challenges simply to stay on task and get that task completed effectively and efficiently. All of which mean that maybe that child with the poor spelling doesn't need extra literacy lessons but extra 'how to organise your literacy, numeracy, science or whatever it is' lessons.

That's a very different challenge from simply giving a child a bit of leeway when it comes to the weekly spelling test.

I have seen this first hand with my eldest daughter as she has struggled through school (or rather struggled through the part of school that makes literacy and numeracy the be-all and the end-all of the whole shooting match. Grrrr ...). She was diagnosed with dyslexia properly at age 11 which meant, at least, we could refer to her as a 'one-armed juggler'. In other words, she was a clever girl working twice as hard as those around her to achieve at school. Well done you! This conceit helped enormously with her self-esteem. After all, almost her entire school career had been a battle for her self-esteem. Imagine going to work every day knowing that practically everything that will be asked of you will make you look stupid and any help you get, if you get any at all, will make you feel even more dumb ('special' lessons, the 'baby' table, staying behind in the exam hall with the 'thick kids' to finish the exam, she's been through it all). But, like so many people with dyslexia, she is far from stupid. (She's currently doing the IB in the VIth form after a year of self study at home. Her learning has come on in leaps and bounds since we prevented teachers from teaching her badly.)

In fact, according to Ronald D. Davis in his book *The Gift of Dyslexia:***

'The mental function that causes dyslexia is a gift in the truest sense of the word: *a natural ability, a talent.* It is something special that enhances the individual.'

The author identifies eight basic abilities shared by dyslexics:

1. They can use the brain's ability to alter and create perceptions (the primary ability)

2. They are highly aware of the environment

3. They are more curious than average

4. They think mainly in pictures instead of words

5. They are highly intuitive and perceptive

6. They think and perceive multidimensionally (using all the senses)

7. They can experience thought as reality

8. They have vivid imaginations

All of which, if it survives the twin attacks of parenting and school, means that the dyslexic adult so often displays 'higher than normal intelligence and extraordinary creative abilities'.

That's a bit different from that thick kid who still can't spell simple words don't you think?

Foreword

The author of the book you now have in your hands is a young man who, like my daughter, has been to a school like yours. It is the story of what went on at such schools combined with advice, strategies and tips about what should have gone on. It's about what dyslexia really is and how frustrating life with it is and how easy it would be for schools to make life better for children with it. And it's written from the point of view of someone who has, as the subtitle suggests, seen life from both sides of the classroom. We hope you will use it to help one-armed jugglers everywhere.

Ian Gilbert
Hong Kong

Chapter 1
Introduction

There are two things I would like to introduce before we continue: the first is myself, because a lot of this book is based on my personal experience, and the second is this book. First things first: I am currently a student studying a Secondary Physical Education teaching degree (QTS) at the

University of Chichester. At age 8 I was diagnosed with dyslexia and dyspraxia. Dyslexia is generally associated with having difficulty learning to read and decoding language although it is far from limited to this. Dyspraxia, on the other hand, is a motor learning difficulty that affects coordination and movements. The two conditions are associated and can often develop together but are not the same.

I progressed through the education system with varied levels of success and support. There were many times when I felt angry and frustrated with my situation and there have been other times when, thanks to the support I received, I managed to achieve things I didn't think would be possible at one stage. Ultimately, for better or for worse, and thanks to the education system and every teacher I have ever had (both good and bad), that is why I have written this book – in the hope that my experience might benefit others. My aim is to try to optimise the educational opportunities and understanding that people with dyslexia receive during their schooling.

This book will grow with age. I start by looking at some of the early signs of dyslexia before progressing through the UK education system and finally on into higher education and what it is like to be on the other side of the classroom. Along the way, drawing on my own experience, I assess what the research tells us and what support is available. I also include some of my own personal hints and tips that you might find useful. Although this book is primarily aimed at teachers, hopefully it will support students and parents alike.

The important thing to bear in mind when approaching dyslexia is that individuals don't either have or not have dyslexia; rather it works on a continuum, and not a simple lateral one at that. People have different severities in different areas and must always be treated as individuals and never tarred with the brush of 'having a condition'. Teaching is incredibly difficult, and if you find it easy then you are a cheat, a liar or in the words of Sir John Jones 'a weaver of magic'![1] It is so important not to make assumptions and jump to conclusions about your students, and yet often we have a limited amount of information to work with and the 'reality' of dealing with what lies in front of us kicks in. To help you take reality and kick it out of the classroom where it belongs, at the end of each chapter I include a 'teacher tips' section which will give you some practical solutions to draw on. My aim is to help you with your 'ACBs', but I don't mean teaching you to read and write. The 'ACBs' I am referring to are these:

A – Assessment

Looking at assessment on a number of levels: assessing for dyslexia, Assessment for Learning in the classroom and how to deal with formal and informal assessments.

C – Classroom practice

Practical and useful strategies to pull out and give a try – and, with a bit of luck, adapt and improve on! This section is at the heart of good quality teaching and learning and will hopefully give you some ideas to help you reflect on your practice, experiment with ideas, take a few risks and above all have fun. These strategies will benefit all young people, not just those with dyslexia.

B – Behaviour

Dyslexia can manifest itself in challenging behaviour, often boredom and the inability to engage with school life, which can then lead to bad behaviour. This section aims to help you spot problems before they get out of hand.

Dyslexia is always there but hopefully these tips will give you a better idea of how to deal with scenarios should they arise. Even while writing this and using a spell-checker, I still needed other people to read and check my work a number of times. Here's an example of some of my most common mistakes:

- *Where* and *were* – both good words when used in the right place but with different meanings.
- *Definitely* – when spell-checked this came out as *defiantly*, giving a totally different meaning.
- *Anachronisms* and *acronyms* are two very different things.
- *Is it* instead of *it is* – two little words, one is a question and the other a statement. Spell-checkers don't identify errors like these.
- *Their/they're*.
- *Your/you're*.

There were a whole host more but I lose track after a while. My favourite mistake however was writing *defecate* rather than *deficit*! You have to be able to laugh at yourself, some-times dyslexia is funny!

Chapter 2
Dys-lex-ia

Writing about dyslexia presents a bit of a challenge. As someone with dyslexia I have the personal experience, but how can I ensure that this comes across in the written word? Conversely, if I wasn't dyslexic, how could I back up what I was writing with experience? How indeed can you help someone without dyslexia to understand what it is like to have the condition, especially when it is so variable?

I was recently asked what it is like for a dyslexic to read. For me, words often appear as broken up rather than fluid, which can lead to a text losing its meaning. Here is how the British Dyslexia Association represents visual stress[2] (please note the distortion is deliberate – there is nothing wrong with the printing!):

Read Regular is created without copying or mirroring shapes. Therefore the frequency of repeated shapes in a text is decreased. This results in a minimum chance of visual distortions (swirl-effect). The aim is to create interesting typography that will maintain the readers' interest and will prevent them from getting bored or frustrated. Diversity in text knows many variations. We must understand the fact that typography for a novel is different from a magazine or a publication for education. Even so a novel has the potential to be clear and interesting. This can be achieved in any level of creativity, thinking on type size, leading, the amount of words on a sentence and the character/paper combination.

Semoteims wehn you are reiadng and the txet deos not folw or you hvae to psaue to raed a wrod it can bomece dfifiluct not jsut to raed but to udenstrnad waht you are redaing and you may lsoe the imacpt of putnuiatcon and hvae to read thnigs sevreal tmies oevr.

In adDition You Sometimes see things Look EXtremely dIfferent As *shown*

This is just to try and give you an idea of what it can be like
rather than an accurate replication. It is also a good
demonstration of how the mind processes words.

These are not literal examples but an attempt to give you
some idea of what it might be like to have difficulties with
reading. What is perhaps harder to put into a usable example
is the difference in how the dyslexic mind processes words.
It is interesting to note that, dyslexic or not, you were probably able to work out what was being said in the above
examples even if it took you slightly longer than usual. This
is all down to that remarkable thing between your ears; not
the hard bony bit but the altogether more squidgy bit in-
between. Somewhere in the brain is the key to understanding
dyslexia – and hopefully this chapter will help you along the
way.

Dyslexia was originally described by the term 'word blindness', which is far from an apt description of the condition
and is probably why it was abandoned. However, the medical
profession could have chosen something easier to spell than
dyslexia! Still, perhaps by the time this book is finished I may
have mastered the spelling at least. Despite the name change,
the idea of 'word blindness' still persists – that dyslexia is the
inability to read.

Worse still is the perception that dyslexia is associated with
the 'less able', which couldn't be further from the truth. Linda
Silverman of the Gifted Development Center has found that

children who tested as gifted also seemed to share a number of learning problems associated with dyslexia.[3] Although not exclusively, many dyslexics tested demonstrate extremely high and above average IQs. Indeed, it is the discrepancy between IQ and levels of reading and writing ability that currently acts as the most used test for dyslexia. As an example, my reading level is below average (98) and my written level is around average (114), however my verbal IQ is quite high (149). That said, it is easier to reach a lot of people with a book than to give you all my phone number! It has been suggested that as some areas of the brain develop considerably better than others, it is the difference in processing speed between the left and right brain that causes problems. The areas in the right side of the brain – associated with conceptualisation and creativity – are considerably quicker than those linked with decoding symbols, such as reading.[4] This is why people with dyslexia can also experience a number of positive traits. For example:

- Their perceptions can be created or altered by the brain (the primary ability).
- They have a high level of environmental awareness.
- They think and perceive multidimensionally (using all the senses).
- They can experience thought as reality.
- They have higher than average levels of curiosity.
- They are visual thinkers.
- They are highly intuitive and insightful.
- They have vivid imaginations.[5]

I wouldn't always consider my dyslexia a 'gift', as Davis and Braun do, but every cloud has a silver lining and it would seem that it can have its benefits. At the very least it somehow landed me a publishing contract, if not just for the irony.

The word dyslexia is derived from two Greek words, *dys* which means 'bad, abnormal or difficult' and *lexis* meaning 'word'. Φοβερό δημιουργικότητα was obviously a bit of a mouthful (for those of you who are a little behind on your Greek humour that translates as 'awesome creativity').

Dyslexia is a learning disability that impacts on the *form* in which information is presented; it not the information itself that is the problem. Dyslexia has an effect on everything from reading, writing and listening to organisation and processing, but specifically not intelligence. It affects people in different ways and it is this large degree of variation which means that, as with all learning, we need to ensure that as teachers we tailor our approach to the individual. This should be a primary consideration throughout this book – many of the strategies may need to be adapted or may not even work for some of your students. It is important to be selective and find what works best for you and them.

Research has highlighted that dyslexia is affected by developmental and genetic characteristics.[6] There is not one gene which is responsible for dyslexia, but a series of genes which can lead to an increased chance of its development. In this respect it is hereditary but not a promise. Dyslexia is a learning difficulty and therefore, like its counterparts, it is a neurological condition. It generally develops in the foetus during pregnancy when the brain gains around a quarter of a million brain cells every minute towards a final total of somewhere in the region of 100 billion.[7] This results in a network of many trillions of connections, which in itself is an inconceivable number, dyslexia or no dyslexia.

As our knowledge of neuroscience develops we are beginning to have a much better understanding of conditions such as dyslexia. Magnetic resonance imaging (MRI) scans reveal that certain areas of the brain, which are known to have a high association with language, seem to light up less in people with dyslexia.[8] It is believed that this is because during brain development these connections do not form in the same way as they do typically. It is difficult however to translate any of this into the real world, other than to give us a better understanding of the origin of the condition and perhaps consider ways to stimulate these areas of the brain in early childhood. Studies have shown that there are windows of opportunity for the optimum development of various aspects of language so it is important that we exploit these opportunities.[9]

Even more fascinating is that when we look at dyslexia globally we that find the condition varies between languages. Different languages are structured in different ways and place different emphasis on different sounds and structures and therefore use different areas of the brain. English turns out to be one of the hardest languages to learn, so perhaps we should teach students a number of languages from an early age to allow them to have more diverse forms of expression. Even more mind-boggling is the notion that if you were born dyslexic in the UK, you might not have been had you been born in Japan, and vice versa. It is all down to the specific areas of the brain which have been shaped and developed during childhood.

When we add reading to the equation it becomes more interesting again. John Stein and Zoi Kapoula suggest that 'more than half of dyslexic children may have eye control problems', a condition that can go on to heighten problems caused by dyslexia.[10] Dyslexics can have difficulties tracking along the page as well as processing the words themselves. If you have been diagnosed with dyslexia it is often recommended that you have your eyes tested. There is not a definite connection but it is always worth checking. It shouldn't be considered as the cause of the problem but rather a catalyst.

Historically visual impairment has often been cited as a root to reading problems[11] and there have even been cases made for visual forms of dyslexia. Johnson and Mylkebust[12] and Boder[13] went on to try to divide dyslexia into auditory and visual categories. Since then a whole range of research has attempted to pinpoint and categorise dyslexia into neat piles. The problem is that it doesn't really fit. Individuals are affected differently and ultimately these nice neat piles end up in a complete mess. It is always important, therefore, to ensure that students with dyslexia are treated as individuals with their own strengths and weaknesses.[14]

It is also worth considering other neurological learning difficulties when thinking about dyslexia. There is a link between dyslexia and dyspraxia, dyscalculia, attention deficit disorder, hyperactivity and the autistic spectrum. The association is not entirely clear, other than that a connection can be drawn between the causes of these conditions and that they affect the working memory (but often in different ways). It is possible that a child with one of these conditions may well have symptoms connected with the others, or even experience one of those conditions as well.[15]

Who is it likely to affect?

Studies suggest that around 10% of the population have signs of dyslexia with around 4% being affected severely.[16] For teachers, this means that there is a good chance that there is at least one pupil in your class with dyslexia, whether they know it or not. Research has shown varying degrees of dyslexia bias towards particular people, but in general it doesn't seem to show any prejudice towards race or economic status (but it does seem to depend on the sample taken). The only area where there has always seemed to be a slight tilt is gender. In 1984 Nathlie Badian did a study which showed that dyslexia was four times more likely in males than females;[17] since then however it has been shown to be a little more balanced.[18] Although I don't believe there is any likelihood of increased levels of dyslexia in males, there is still some significance because it is often easier to spot in boys.

In order to explain myself on this point I will refer to the sometimes controversial work of James Flynn on intelligence and gender difference.[19] When we look at average IQ scores, women have gained on men in the last decade to be equal or even a point or two ahead. Before you start to feel smug or hard done by, depending on your gender, what is interesting about the difference is that there is no correlation with genetic superiority. Flynn puts the difference down to the ability of girls to engage in mental exercises at school. But what is more remarkable is the social and cultural impact on IQ. Flynn found that female university students had a lower average IQ than their male counterparts; however, they were still able to get the required grades at school and university because they were better at engaging with schoolwork. The nature of the work itself also had an impact: female students seemed to engage better with the academic work generally demanded in schools and universities. This could be a contributing reason as to why we might notice dyslexia more easily in boys – when you add dyslexia to the equation boys are even less likely to get on with academic work.

What is also worth noting about Flynn's work is how these cultural impacts might have an impact in your classroom. In his book *Asian Americans*, Flynn looks at the potential difference between Asian-American and white students.[20] He finds that, academically, a Chinese student with a comparable IQ to their white counterpart will in all likelihood do better in their academic grades – which could be down to the fact that academia is highly valued by their parents and culture. So, perhaps a cultural change in our classrooms could lead to better results. However, China also has the highest teenage suicide rate, which is also put down to academic pressure, so we do need to find a healthy balance.

Chapter 3
The Early Years

According to my mum I arrived in the world three-and-a-half weeks early and I have been making up for it ever since. I was long and skinny, rather bruised and battered, missing most of my toenails and somewhat hairy; none of which has really changed, apart from the addition of toenails! Within the first 48 hours of life I was diagnosed with severe jaundice and spent my first fortnight under an ultraviolet light, only being taken out to be fed and changed. Once home I proved to be a demanding baby, not sleeping much (something which has changed) and always after attention (something which hasn't). By around ten months I'd had a short spell in hospital with a virus and soon after that cleared I began to settle.

I did not walk until I was 15 months old, despite brave efforts to keep up with my older brother, Sam, who was 14 months ahead of me. It was always said that Sam had read the baby book before he was born and followed it to the letter, while I threw the book out and improvised. Potty-training and talking came relatively slowly, which I now know is most likely due to the fact that muscle control and muscle tension takes longer to develop in children with dyspraxia. In addition, the NHS notes that during the early years it is common for children with dyslexia to miss normal stages of development such as sitting, standing, toilet-training and walking.[21] In the later stages of development there can be problems with gross motor skills and the more fine motor skills, such as writing. Both children with dyslexia and/or dyspraxia can find it difficult to replicate movements and they may find it hard to focus and concentrate at times. This is probably largely due to the connection between dyslexia, dyspraxia and Attention Deficit Disorder (ADD).[22]

With two boys just over a year apart, my poor mum decided that the best strategy was lots of trips to the park, a wide variety of toys and plenty of mess! I think this is actually a great approach for supporting any child's development, but it was particularly good for me. We climbed, jumped, swung, kicked and threw about just about everything. We were fortunate to have a big garden, a climbing frame, a slide and ride-on toys.

When I was 15 months old, mum went back to work part-time and I spent a lot of time with my Aunty Jen where I had two older cousins to contend with. I was now attempting to keep up with both of them as well as with my older brother. This constant interaction with older children helped me a great deal as I was always pushing myself trying to be like them. By the time I was 2 years old I went to nursery with my brother, and mum was back to work full-time. The nursery was very good with lots of structured and free-flow play which suited me well – I loved any opportunity to make a mess and get stuck in.

One of my favourite stories from this time was of making Christmas cards – we did a reindeer with hand prints for antlers. My brother refused to put his hands in the paint until he had a bowl of soapy water ready to dunk them into when he had finished, whereas I was content to get myself, and everything around me, covered in paint at the earliest opportunity. I believe that this type of engagement and motivation for practical tasks is probably quite typical for many children but particularly for those with dyslexia. Good quality early years education is essential for dyslexics and dyspraxics because it is holistic and encompasses fine and gross motor skills along with the development of language and communication. This type of broad approach is engaging for children and allows for the development of a wide range of skills – everything from the core skills of language and motor development right through to creativity, empathy, problem-solving and social skills.

My transition from nursery to reception went smoothly and was relatively successful at first. I attended an infant school where the early years were particularly strong. I started part-time for the first term before going full-time in the second term. The school offered lots of interaction and plenty of practical activities. One example activity was the use of small sand trays which we could draw in and begin to experiment with forming letters and writing. It worked particularly well because not only did you get the feel for what you were doing and an idea of letter shapes, but it was instantly erasable and you could get in lots of practice. This sort of approach – which allows for easy correction and plenty of mistakes, while still being very interactive and practical – is perfect and suited me well. Other examples included using beads and colours to learn patterns and develop basic numeracy.

It was at this stage that some of the early indications of my dyslexia became more apparent. When writing or drawing I would use either hand or often swap hands from one side of the page to another – a habit which I actually wish I had never got out of, as being ambidextrous could have been quite useful. Other signs included the way I gripped a pen, which was unorthodox and changeable, and I couldn't maintain an even pressure. These basic coordination problems continued through to other tasks. One day I even managed to cut a hole in my shirt after having moved the scissors all the way round the paper until I was cutting towards myself, instead of turning the paper. None of these signals are conclusive in themselves – plenty of children in their early years will display fine and gross motor coordination challenges. It is only when you look back that you see them as indications of something bigger.

What are the early signs?

The chance of being able to spot dyslexia in the early years is very rare. It can be hereditary so if you are a parent and have been diagnosed yourself, or even if you think you might fit the description but have never been tested, it is certainly something you should look out for in your children.

There are a number of websites which list some of the indications most commonly seen in the early stages of development, but they are far from a sure-fire diagnostic tool. The fact is that at this age there isn't a definitive test for dyslexia. All you can do as a teacher or parent is keep your eyes peeled for any clues. With that in mind it is worth keeping track of how your child learns best and some of their tendencies.

The British Dyslexia Association provides the following list of some problems to look out for:

- Has difficulty learning nursery rhymes.

- Finds difficulty paying attention, sitting still and listening to stories.

- Likes listening to stories but shows no interest in letters or words.

- Has difficulty learning to sing or recite the alphabet.

- Has a history of slow speech development.

- Gets words muddled (e.g. cubumber, flutterby).

- Has difficulty keeping a simple rhythm.

- Finds it hard to carry out two or more instructions at one time (e.g. Put the toys in the box then put it on the shelf) but is fine if tasks are presented in smaller units.

- Forgets names of friends, teachers, colours, etc.

- Poor auditory discrimination.

- Finds difficulty cutting, sticking and crayoning in comparison with their peer group.

- Has persistent difficulty in dressing (e.g. finds shoelaces and buttons difficult).

- Puts clothes on the wrong way round.

- Has difficulty with catching, kicking or throwing a ball.

- Often trips, bumps into things or falls over.

- Has difficulty hopping or skipping.

- Has obvious 'good' and 'bad' days for no apparent reason.[23]

Looking through this list I could probably tick off a whole host of these, but it is not necessarily all-encompassing of the condition. At this early stage, the rate of children's development varies a lot so it is often hard to tell. Dyslexia is something which is definitely worth bearing in mind as a teacher or parent, but as long as your children are at a good early years establishment and are kept active and have a smile on their face, then try not to worry too much for now.

What support is available?

If a diagnosis is made then the support at this stage can be very good. In the UK, legislation laid out by government, such as the Early Years Foundation Stage (EYFS) guidance and the national curriculum, highlights key areas for educational establishments to focus on alongside a wide range of targets. The emphasis is very much on the individual child's needs and the EYFS Statutory Framework specifically mentions that any learning difficulties should be provided for with appropriate and adaptive practice.[24] The Framework deals with any pupils up to the age of 5 and largely allows for early years providers to make decisions about how to best approach achieving these goals. This is ideal for formulating the perfect learning environment for any child but also serves children with dyslexia particularly well. There is a focus on ensuring that children remain engaged and enjoy learning, but there is no formal testing – the programme relies on Assessment for Learning and day-to-day observations. This tailored approach means that it should be possible to meet every pupil's needs. As a teacher you have the freedom to adapt your practice to the individual. Parents should work closely with schools to find what works best for their child and make sure that both teachers and the school or nursery is well informed as to their child's particular requirements.

In terms of getting advice about dyslexia there are hundreds of books and websites with a wealth of information. Some good places to begin (apart from this book of course) include:

- British Dyslexia Association – www.bdadyslexia.org.uk
- Dyslexia the Gift – www.dyslexia.com
- Learning Disabilities Worldwide – www.ldworldwide.org
- Dyslexia My Life – http://dyslexiamylife.org
- Young minds – www.youngminds.org.uk

Teacher tips

A – Assessment

Observation and record-keeping of children's behaviour and engagement is essential. Photos and sticky notes are a helpful way to keep track of their key behaviours, strengths/weaknesses and areas for development. A comment in a notebook or on a computer works equally well but ensure that it is in a place where it can be easily used, referred to and updated. It is important that you are keeping track. This record will not only give you a clear picture of progress but also allow you to plan the best programme of help in the future.

Focus on fine and gross motor skills in your record-keeping: what does the child find easy or difficult? It doesn't have to be complicated but an individual tracking system can help to identify problem behaviours early on. I would also suggest that this information is passed on in some form to parents and other teachers – it can be really helpful in preventing teachers (and students) from having to start from square one every term or school year, and will give everyone a frame of reference.

C – Classroom practice

It is important to have a hands-on and tactile approach to learning at this early age. Not only does it make activities more interesting and engaging but it really helps the development of fine motor skills. I have included a few of my favourite ideas.

Fine motor skills

- Sand tray – Use sand trays for both writing and drawing to see what the children can create with their hands. You can develop this further by using different objects to write with, each time getting one step closer to using a pen or pencil.

- Counting with beads – You can use ideas such as jewellery-making and so forth to help children learn counting and patterns. You don't necessarily have to use beads – anything with a bit of colour can be used to form a pattern; perhaps you could build a house with different coloured bricks!

- Finger/hand-painting – Try getting the children to paint on various objects with different surfaces and textures or experiment with mixing sand into the paint.

- Water play – Water is another great tactile substance, and the best part is it just dries up when you're done!

Gross motor skills

- ▓ Climbing – On anything and everything!
- ▓ It's a fine balance – Try using balance boards or beams and benches.
- ▓ Movement – Bikes, trikes and ride-on toys.

Basically all of the messy fun stuff! As a basic rule of thumb incorporate lots of exploration, make it clear that mistakes help learning and generally encourage a 'can do' and 'have a go' attitude.

B – Behaviour

Challenging behaviour can crop up quite commonly among dyslexic children. It can affect individuals in different ways but I think there is a definite link between having difficulty communicating your emotions and becoming disengaged with your work and looking for distractions. For that reason it pays to have some strategies up your sleeve. Try out the following.

- ▓ You've got a friend in me – Encourage socialisation. Simple things like sharing and turn-taking are really important and children can learn a lot about the right way to behave from their peers.
- ▓ Talk the talk – It is essential that children know how to express themselves. Language development and good communication skills will help to alleviate the frustration of not being able to articulate clearly, something that can

lead to physical communication of the wrong sort! Setting a good example is always a good way to start and then making sure you back this up by showing that you really value this type of behaviour in your classroom.

Chapter 4
Primary School

My earliest memories of the education system are very disjointed. When I look back, I remember struggling a great deal through infant and junior school. But the cracks really began to show when I got to Year 3, moving from Key Stage 1 to Key Stage 2. These transitions are always difficult and the education system doesn't manage them particularly well. A change of environment and a shift in the focus for learning – becoming more focused around written output – doesn't favour children with learning difficulties and they can often become disengaged.

My biggest issue was now self-esteem. I was now old enough to recognise that there was a difference between my 'perceived' ability and the ability of those around me. This was most notable with my aptitude for reading which I remember being distinctly lower than my peers. On top of this the written work I produced was barely legible – my spelling was poor, as was my grammar. The difficulties I was having at school inevitably led to me being tested by an occupational therapist, which is one of my earliest memories. I remember playing with balls, doing spelling and wondering what it was all about. The outcome of this was a report which showed that I had both dyslexia and dyspraxia. Surprisingly the report also indicated that I had quite good gross motor skills for my age (e.g. throwing and catching) but contrastingly poor fine motor skills (e.g. writing). This was probably largely down to having a sport-mad family, something which I think helped me a great deal to meet the challenge of my dyspraxia and dyslexia.

I started school when I was 4 years and 9 months old. The fact that I was an autumn-born baby was an advantage because it gave me a bit of extra time to adapt. The largest group on the special educational needs (SEN) register are summer-born children and I don't think it is a coincidence – age definitely makes a difference.

I was first tested for dyslexia and dyspraxia in 1997 when I was 8 years old. This led to some improvements in terms of empowering my family to gain further support from the school and from suggestions within the report on how to improve my development. The full report makes an interesting read and I would like to include a few extracts as I think it represented a real turning point in the support I was given: 'Joseph presented a friendly, tall, slim 8 year old, who was willing to attempt all that was asked of him.' My strengths included a 'friendly personality, good sense of humour, good imagination and he is inventive'. I had some trouble with 'writing, sustained concentration, achieving his potential in school and sports [and] emotional control at times'. It goes on to explain that I lacked confidence and could become overanxious. I was also distractible, attention-seeking and became easily frustrated with activities. I dare say that I would still be many of those things if it wasn't for the measures put in place to support me. Jill Christmas, who wrote the report, suggests a wide variety of support from playing the drums to help my coordination to foam pen grips. She also recommended learning to touch-type to cope with the increased amount of written work I would need to do. There was even an emphasis placed on raising my self-esteem through structured day-to-day activities. These full reports are extremely useful for teachers and parents as they are very much tailored to the individual child. If you have a pupil who has yet to get one then I implore you to pursue this avenue. (There are more details on the process in the teacher tips at the end of this chapter.)

However, when I look back I can't help but feel that the education system failed me in a number of ways at this time.

The focus was always on my weaknesses and not my strengths. Rather than trying to ensure work was accessible for me, barriers were constantly thrown up – and my inability to clamber over them was highlighted time and time again. Perhaps this is where my frustration with tasks came in, something had been highlighted in the occupational therapist's report.

The most revealing example, one which has stuck with me, is the 'almighty pen licence'. This allowed pupils to progress from writing in pencil to being allowed to use a pen. This could be a real hurdle in the world of primary school and is something which many children with dyslexia find incredibly challenging, including myself. It is a nice idea in principle: once you can write neatly in pencil you receive a beautiful printed certificate and are given your very own handwriting pen. For me this resulted in a complete 'hissy fit': I never thought I would get there because most of my work looked like a spider had crawled across the page.

This is just one instance of the ways in which children with dyslexia can be inadvertently made to feel different and less able because of their difficulties with written work. Along with weekly spelling tests, which I dreaded, and constantly handing in work that I could never be really proud of, I can attest to feeling alienated on a number of levels. This is a problem that I imagine a lot of children experience, but especially those with dyslexia, diagnosed or not. The huge emphasis on written work in exercise books does not help to grow confidence or capacity. In contrast, being able to present work in a variety of ways – spoken, written, in groups, visually, recorded, produced on computer – can all help to boost self-esteem.

Key Stages 1 and 2 are vital time in a child's development, so I think there is a real need for change in the way the school system operates. The problem is that if pupils can't engage with what they are learning at the most fundamental level, i.e. its format, then it is extremely likely that they will be put off the rest of the work. This issue needs to be addressed on two levels. Firstly, the manner in which we teach needs to be extended. Although fundamental skills such as language are important, there are a number of ways in which it can be used and expressed. The primary focus of a dynamic and skills-based learning environment should be to ensure that work is engaging and relevant to the pupils.

Secondly, we need to consider what we value in the education system and what we want to assess. While it may be beneficial for a child to write neatly and coherently, if they can demonstrate these same skills in another way, such as verbally, then this should be valued equally. It is important to look to the future: there aren't many people who write for a living. Even though many may use e-mail and the like, they do not rely only on this as a sole means of communication. There are certainly very few that actually use handwriting in their day-to-day work – even doctors have moved to electronic prescriptions! The working world has moved to the digital age and the classroom needs not only to follow but attempt to be one step ahead. This is easier said than done but nonetheless it should still be our ultimate goal, especially when you consider the claim by the Department of Education that of those children currently in Year 5 at school, when they enter employment 80% of them will be in a job that hasn't been invented yet.[25] If part of our role as teachers is to prepare children for their future life, then how do we do this when the world is changing so rapidly and we don't really have a clear idea of what we are preparing them for?

How does this all realistically translate into what we do in the classroom? Well, first and foremost as teachers, parents and pupils, we need to be demanding an up-to-date or even future-focused learning experience from our schools, instead of a narrow focus on exam results. In addition we need a unified approach to any obstacles – the pupils at the forefront supported by teachers and parents who communicate with each other to provide the best assistance possible. By this I mean learning tailored to the pupils' needs with teachers and parents sharing information to formulate the best support for that particular child. When I was at school I was fortunate enough to have a mother who worked in the education system and she did exactly that, but if you are not so lucky to be involved in the wonderful world of education it can be hard to know where to start. My advice as a teacher is simple: (1) establish good communication with the child and make sure they know you are on their side, (2) when you talk about the child's education ensure they are involved in the conversation, (3) be prepared to challenge anything that you don't think is right, (4) talk to the school and the parents about what the child *can do* and is *good at* and (5) check the parents know what they can do at home to support their child's learning. Be realistic but optimistic.

In 2003 Leon Feinstein did some research on how socio-economic class could affect educational development.[26] What is interesting about his findings (see figure below) is that those from a low social class show significant decline or lack of development in comparison to those from a high social class. This is largely attributed to differences in upbringing: those from a high social class with a supportive family had approximately a 4:1 ratio of positive reinforcement to negative; that ratio is reversed for their counterparts from a low social class. Significantly, it has also been shown that children from more privileged backgrounds hear up to 32 million more words than their counterparts and therefore develop a wider vocabulary than their counterparts.[27]

So, when it comes to entering school, there is already a difference in children's moral reasoning and motivation, depending on the social and economic status. This is described by Lawrence Kohlberg in his theory of moral development:[28]

Level 1 (pre-conventional): negative reinforcement

1. Obedience and punishment orientation (How can I avoid punishment?)

2. Self-interest orientation (What's in it for me?)

Level 2 (conventional): positive reinforcement

3. Interpersonal accord and conformity (the good boy/good girl attitude)

4. Authority and social-order maintaining orientation (law and order morality)

Children's understanding of the world around them progresses rapidly at this age. What occurs in this key period can impact directly on their subsequent intelligence, educational achievement and behaviour. So it is important to do as much as we can to ensure that we have a unified approach at home and in school. It is entirely possible that dyslexia could be attributed to problems that emerge in these early stages of development.

I would like to emphasise the need for positivity at this stage. At this period in their lives children are formulating a mass of memories which could greatly impact the rest of their lives. It is important that they aren't given a negative 'label', so it is fundamental to stress the idea that dyslexia can be something that we value positively as a society and balance this against the strengths and weaknesses that it can bring.

Are schools and teachers too quick to reach a judgement and give it a label? Does that then excuse our teaching methods and conceal the shortcomings in our dealings with certain children, rather than meeting the learning needs of all the pupils in our care? We need to ask ourselves some tough questions and strive to seek answers in an open and honest way. I recently attended a PE conference in Kent at which Dame Tanni Grey-Thompson was the keynote speaker. During her presentation she displayed a picture of herself in her Brownie uniform in her wheelchair with a skipping rope! She said that as a child growing up no one ever told her 'you can't do that' but always encouraged her to 'have a go' at whatever she wanted to do. Look what she has gone on to achieve! This sort of approach could revolutionise our educational practice and challenge our national cultural norms so that we focus on strengths and not weaknesses.

Thinking Actively in a Social Context (TASC) is a particularly good model for child development as it combines core skills and subjects with the social and emotional aspects of learning.[29] It works well in helping children to learn in a number of different ways. The TASC website (www.tascwheel.com) provides a whole host of ideas, many of which are quite dyslexia-friendly, so it is a great place to start.

The Times Educational Supplement online (www.tes.co.uk/teaching-resource/Early-Learning-Goals-3007398) also has a range of materials; some better than others, but it is certainly worth a look if you are struggling for ideas. Another good resource for helping your pupils become more effective learners (learning to learn) and setting them up for success is Guy Claxton's Building Learning Power (www.buildinglearning-power.co.uk).

Teacher tips

A – Assessment

I am not a huge fan of mass testing but if done well it can be a brilliant way of getting some early indications of learning difficulties, as long as you don't become reliant on it as a method. Keep testing short and simple and then follow it up thoroughly.

A straightforward set of questions can help to indicate if there might be dyslexic tendencies, for example:

■ Do you have difficulty telling left from right?

■ Do you find it hard to remember things that you have just read?

- Do you dislike reading aloud?
- Do you find it difficult to do sums in your head, without using paper or your fingers?
- Is it hard to read your handwriting?
- Do you find it difficult to remember long numbers, like a telephone number?
- Do you find your times tables hard?

I recommend coupling simple questions like these with some basic exercises. These are best done verbally, although you may use spelling tests to assess general spelling ability. Number repetition can also be used to assess short-term memory; this involves saying a series of evenly spaced numbers and pausing before the child repeats them back to you. You can also test phonological processing (how well we process sounds) by asking students to break up words into sounds (e.g. *given* can be split into give-en, so you might ask '*Given* without *give* would leave ...?').

All of these methods can give us a general indication of dyslexia. However, if this is something you feel is worth implementing seriously in your school then it is worth considering purchasing dyslexia tests. Lucid Research (www.lucid-research.com) and GL Assessment (www.gl-assessment.co.uk) both offer computerised testing with instant feedback, while Hodder Tests (www.hoddertests.co.uk) and Pearson Assessment (www.pearsonclinical.co.uk) offer non-computerised testing. Please bear in mind that any testing should be followed up by a consultation with a qualified professional.

Full testing allows for a much more comprehensive view of a child's specific learning needs and is highly recommended if dyslexia has been diagnosed; the more you know, the better equipped you are to tackle the problem. Your special educational needs coordinator should have a lot more knowledge on the subject of further testing and can recommend (with parental consent) that students undertake a full assessment with the local education authority. The process can be very long-winded and difficult but, under the terms of the 2005 Disability Discrimination Act, anyone in full-time education is entitled to a dyslexia assessment.

When I was initially recommended for testing there were no NHS occupational therapists in Kent and the waiting list to see one was between 18 and 24 months. Eventually my parents made the decision to go private. The ensuing report completed by Jill Christmas opened up a lot more support at school, as it contained not only advice but a request that they put further measures of support in place. It also led to a range of helpful suggestions – including one to play the drums to help with my coordination!

The benefit of getting the testing done privately is that it can be put into effect immediately so, if necessary, it may be worthwhile recommending this option to parents. There is usually a cost involved of between £100 and £400. Various charities also offer assessments which can also be considered. There are a number of places where you can find additional support. Your local dyslexia association may be able to direct you to assessors in your area (see www.bdadyslexia.org.uk/

membership/directories/lda-directory.html for a list of local agencies) and charities such as Dyslexia Action (www.dys-lexiaaction.org.uk) can provide further advice. The British Psychological Society (www.bps.org.uk) provides a full list of chartered psychologists.

The real test in all of these scenarios is to make sure you know what you are testing your students for and what the tests are telling you. For example, we often look at a child's reading age. This may give us an idea of how well a child can articulate words but does it tell us how well they understand the concepts involved? Although this sort of information can be very useful, we should ensure that we are not over-reliant on these results and have an idea of the full picture. This broad approach may even lead us to discovering dyslexia – for example, if we notice that a child's understanding is ahead of their reading age. It is important therefore to assess your students in numerous different ways, including verbal, practical and written.

I always hated spelling tests; not only was I not very good at them but they just seemed boring. Although I think it is beneficial to measure spelling ability, there are a variety of ways to do this. For example, we can disguise the spelling test and combine it with a range of other tests, such as a spelling obstacle course where pupils spell different words at various points as they work their way around the course. Or you could tell a story using a word theme (e.g. 'I *like* to ride my *bike*,' said *Mike*, so the students spell all the 'ike' words). You could also use pictures rather than simply reading the words out or maybe use a game of spelling Pictionary. Be creative and make it as interesting as possible – you will still find out how well they can spell.

C – Classroom practice

- The go-to-gear tray – One of the best ideas is to have a tray or area which is full of useful tools and resources which children can draw on at their own instigation (e.g. pencil/pen grips, coloured overlays, lesson specific resources (large print worksheets etc.), alternative scissors, reading rulers, doodle books, stress balls). In this way pupils can really begin to gain some independence and take control of their own learning. Research shows that children really like this idea and they are more likely to use the available resources if they are presented in this way.[30]

- Dyslexia display board – This is an area for staff, pupils and parents to display up-to-date information about dyslexia. It is also a space where pupils can raise awareness about dyslexia for the whole school. When Sheppard and Thorburn-Shears tried this they found that students had lots of good ideas, including highlighting popular celebrities with dyslexia. It is a great way of raising awareness and getting dyslexia out in the open. In this way we can stop dyslexia from being a condition that pupils feel ashamed about to something they are almost proud of, as they should be!

B – Behaviour

- Don't make assumptions – It is easy to draw quick conclusions: the smart child who comes across well verbally but then falls short when it comes to putting their work on paper = lazy and poorly behaved. Keep tabs and look for some clues before you make assumptions; you can always follow up with some further testing.

- Variety is the spice of life – Mix up your tasks and try to teach in a variety of different ways and using a range of learning styles. In terms of targeting those children who may have dyslexia, I would suggest always trying to have a practical and engaging element to tasks.

- Affirmation – There is a lot to be said for the power of the affirmation process, if you take the time to invest in it. The basic idea is to take something that you feel you're not very good at, think about how you want to change it and then simply persuade yourself that you have! It might sound a bit backwards but often the biggest thing stopping you from following through with something is your attitude towards it.

For example, a child might be shy and lacking in confidence. When asked what they could do to appear more confident they might say 'I could put my hand up in class more'. They could then make the affirmation that 'I am very confident because I put my hand up in class'. Or a child may have a temper and say 'I need more patience'. They could do this by counting if they start to feel angry. Their affirmation might be: 'I am a very patient person because I just count whenever I start to feel angry'.

The objective is to use the affirmation to empower yourself by repeating it on a regular basis and reinforcing it. There are two ways in which this can work really well. Firstly, your students could use it themselves as a way to set personal goals – it is a little bit different so hopefully they will show some interest. It sets a clear target, with a definite way of marking achievement and, most importantly, it actually gives students the belief in themselves to achieve it. The second way is through you as a teacher, especially when it comes to behavioural problems. Instead of 'Oh Billy, you really need to stop flicking all the girls in the ear!' or 'Oh not again Billy', you need to put a positive spin on everything (think like a politician!). When you tell kids off in this negative manner you just reinforce the idea that they are 'bad'; if I tell you that you are naughty enough times you will start to believe it. Instead try: 'Oh Billy, I never had you down as an ear flicker – you're always so well-behaved and work really hard for me!' so Billy knows that he has done something wrong but at the same time you are implanting this little seed of an idea that he is actually a 'good boy'. Focus on the behaviour you *do* want and don't emphasise the behaviour you *don't* want.

Chapter 5
Secondary School

The part of Kent where I grew up was an area where the 11-plus was – and still is – used to decide whether pupils go to a selective grammar school or a non-selective high school. I didn't get on well with exams at this age and fell just under the pass mark. This meant I attended a nearby secondary school, a co-educational high school; my brother went to the boys grammar school which was next door.

My experience of secondary school was very mixed. It was the kind of school where instead of rubbers being thrown across the classroom, chairs were. My schooling was patchy because it was such a challenging environment; some teachers did very well, some just managed the situation and others had no control whatsoever. In terms of assistance, I went to learning support during class times two or three times a week. On the whole this was not a great system for me: firstly because I had terrible organisational skills and would often forget that I was supposed to go, and secondly because I was missing out on lessons (although that didn't always seem like such a bad thing at the time). On the other hand, I was taught how to touch-type which is perhaps one of the most valuable skills that I possess. I not only use it on an almost daily basis now but it enables me to produce presentable work which I can instantly change, rearrange and edit as much as needed. However, one year into secondary school my parents decided that this wasn't the best environment for me because they could see that I was not progressing at an appropriate rate, that my needs were not really being met and that the quality of teaching was questionable.

My sister had started to attend a small local independent school and was now in Year 3. Knowing that she was getting on well there they decided to send me to an open-day at the same school. It was an odd experience and a complete contrast to what I had been used to, but it was definitely an improvement. I joined the school for the last few weeks of Year 7 so that I wouldn't be stepping into completely foreign territory come September, something which definitely eased the transition. I found the smaller classes of only 18 or 20 pupils not only made life easier for me but also for the teachers, which benefited everyone. The school was also much smaller with only two classes in my year. This made it simple to find my way around and get to know my environment and the people in it better.

Eager to impress, I found myself working incredibly hard and achieving well through Year 8. The school worked with my parents to provide the right sort of help. I went to learning support a few times a week but, importantly, this was during registration to avoid being pulled out from classes. Whilst there I would be able to talk through any problems I was having and we developed coping strategies. Having spent a lot of time doing handwriting exercises by now I despised them and explained that I didn't think working on my reading and writing was helping me. To my surprise, after a while, I was listened to. The point was to concentrate on the aspects that I could control and was good at rather than going over the same old exhausted process. In my first year I did quite well and got myself full house colours and a minor scholarship. Although in the years to follow I began to become disengaged with some of the academic work and the teaching style that can sometimes be found in more traditional independent schools, on the whole it was a good experience for me.

The key points that I would take from this experience as a teacher today is that you should grasp any opportunity you have to get to know your students. One of the best tips I ever got as a student teacher was to seek out pupils at breaktime and lunchtime and get to know them. It is so much easier to teach when you don't have a blindfold on! I also think it is extremely important to listen to what your students are saying about their own learning. During my own schooling I'd felt that I was wasting my time on what I considered to be boring and pointless reading and writing practice. I may have been wrong – possibly it would have been beneficial to do those exercises – but the fact is that I felt so negatively about them there was no way I would engage and so no progress could be made. In that sense at least it was of much more benefit to adapt and try out some different approaches. While your students may not always be right, it is really useful to know what they are thinking.

Although at this stage there was no direct funding or support for my dyslexia, my parents managed to find enough money to buy me a laptop which I was allowed to use during lessons for making notes and producing homework. It proved a very useful tool. However, there now is a lot more help available than just word processing (see Chapter 6).

By Year 9 I was really starting to take control and have an input into the support I received, which was very important to me. Teachers and parents need to provide assistance but ultimately it is down to what works for the individual child, so they need to be at the heart of the decision-making process. A sense of ownership is essential to dealing with your own dyslexia problems. It is all too easy to feel as if much of what happens is outside your control or that you are fighting a losing battle. The key is to identify systems and strategies which *you* can put into place to work around these problems so that you don't feel like you are struggling to stay afloat all the time. There were two factors which really helped me. Firstly, there was the undeniable organisational force that is my mother. She employed everything from white-boards in my room to setting out reminders, endless lists and sticky notes, through to staying in touch with the school to ensure the support was there. Secondly, I had help at school from a teacher who took on the role of my 'organisational mentor'; between him and a few of my friends I was always up to speed with what needed doing and was getting it done. I often went to see him at lunch and breaktime when I could check that my books where tidy and in order and that I knew what homework I had and was on top of it. I could talk about what I had on and think about how I was going to manage my time, all this whilst often listening to Bob Dylan or having my friends watch *Superman* while I organised myself. It was a great way of getting some one-on-one time and having someone to talk to who would point me in the right direction and avoid those 'oops' moments. This tech-nique was employed after several bits of paper flew out of my exercise book at a parents evening due to the amount of work I had done either on handouts or on computer, some-thing which was a bugbear of the teacher in question who then offered his service to ensure that this didn't happen in future. From here the simple act of sticking work into my book meant, when it came to reviewing it or doing revision, all the relevant information was in the right place (well mostly). Receiving support from these key people in my life was invaluable; it is a set-up that I would recommend for anyone who struggles with problems of this nature, dyslexic or not.

Getting organised

If you hadn't already worked it out, I am terrible at getting organised. If you could lose it I probably would; if it could be forgotten then, er, I forget what comes next ... Fear not, however, because there are a few strategies you can employ to help your students to help themselves.

Dear diary ... where are you?

A diary or planner is a great idea and is something most schools provide for their students. I never liked using mine because I had to write in it. However, if you can get past that barrier then the diary can be a useful tool. I preferred to go the electronic way – I now plan everything on my phone. Not only did I find the calendar easier to use but I always had my phone on me and was much better at looking after it than my diary because I was fonder of it! There is so much technology in a mobile phone these days, so it is a shame that as teachers we don't tap into them more (although I know of teachers who have used them to provide music for dance lessons and even video feedback).

One of the other bonuses about using my mobile as a calendar was that it prompted me with reminders and could sync with my online calendar. (Try setting up a simple online email account (e.g. Google Mail) and then sync a mobile phone calendar with it.) I can envisage a school system that works in a similar way: a central calendar that can sync with students' mobiles and home computers. It would certainly challenge most school IT guys and network managers to set up a whole-school integrated system for staff and students alike. Students, parents and teachers could all ensure that things are staying organised and that all the deadlines and reminders are in one place. Schools produce paper diaries for pupils, so why not create an electronic version?

Note to self: find that other note you wrote about the really important thing ...

Everyone has their own little ways to remind themselves of those important things; I prefer to rely on several. There are literally hundreds of techniques to try – just find out what works for your students. Here are a few suggestions.

- The classic string around your wrist – Simply tie a piece of string around your wrist to jog your memory; if you can't remember, then panic!
- The ever-powerful sticky note – Simple but effective; stick them on everything and hopefully you might spot one of them.
- Set a reminder or an alarm on your phone – If it starts buzzing then get busy.

- Whiteboard/blackboard – Get one up on the wall and scribble down what you need to remember, or just doodle on it.
- Note board – Pin your reminders to your heart's content.
- Dictaphone – Leave yourself a message at the beep.
- Organisation – there really is an app for that (see p. 81).

These may sound basic but sometimes simple is best. Encourage your students to try them out and see what works – if they are anything like me they will probably find that they'll end up using a combination of all of the above.

The good, the bad and the ugly

I am sure there are times when I have been extremely frustrating to my parents and teachers alike. In fact, now I think about it, I'm certain (when I lost my first mobile phone down the loo my parents were a bit annoyed; it was a brand new Motorola and it had a radio function as well!). I was often told that I had two speeds – 'dead slow' and 'stop' – and that I could 'sleep for Britain'. The problem was that even the simplest things required a great deal of concentration, so I became tired and lost focus easily. I am also incredibly clumsy and have always had a knack for losing and forgetting things, despite my mum's best efforts to label the world. The trouble is that no matter how irritating it can be as a teacher or parent, you can guarantee it is just as frustrating for the child, if not more so.

As a teacher there are certain tasks which are bound to create problems and should be avoided at all costs. Possibly the most unhelpful thing to do is to ask students to copy from a textbook or off the board. If we aren't careful, it can take a dyslexic child half the lesson just to get the learning objective down! In fact, who really learns anything by copying? Why not just talk to the person next to you about the learning objective instead: What do you think it means? Do you think you will meet it? How do you think you can meet it? What else might you learn today? Why do we always have to use learning objectives anyway – what has happened to spontaneous learning and just following a line of enquiry?

Children with dyslexia become masters of avoidance tactics or 'lastminute.com' experts. If there is something I'm worried about or not sure that I want to do, I will always find something, anything which needs to be done before it. Work with your dyslexic students to improve their advance planning. Remember that any written work will take longer and may need additional support with planning. Typically, the hand of a child with dyslexia will not work anywhere near as quickly as their brain and thoughts; by using mind maps (see p. 69), bullet points and so on to capture the main points you will help them to complete work more successfully and fulfil their full potential. It may even be worth taking the time to call home once in a while, this way you can confirm that the right resources are in place and that progress is being made there as well as in the classroom – consider it a two pronged attack! Consistency is important and its effect is even better if it is reinforced in domestic life, this will enable the child to develop and maintain good habits and routines.

For teachers, as for parents, the worst thing you can do is over-compensate and do too much for the child. It is so easy to get caught up in trying to help them; sometimes the hardest thing to do is step back and let them make mistakes and learn how to help themselves. The ultimate goal should be for parents and schools to support children with dyslexia to develop strategies for themselves and to manage themselves. But by all means encourage them to be tidy, check up on their progress and implement reward systems; set realistic targets for them rather than just thinking it won't happen. Patience is crucial. Just give them the tools to be successful and let them get there on their own (perhaps with a small nudge in the right direction). Good communication is also essential: talk to your child about their day and chat with them about yours; it will give them a chance to reflect on what has happened and reinforce their learning – they might even remember their homework!

Teacher tips

A – Assessment

■ Tools of the trade – During major exams, students with learning difficulties often have access to alternative methods such as readers or computers or are given extra time. It is worth exploring every avenue and ensuring that pupils are given the best possible chance to access these tools when they really need them. It is also important that they get an opportunity to learn how to use them in advance. That means that in the same way that you might do mock examinations, students need to be able to practise taking advantage of the support they need on the big day.

■ Quick assessment – Whenever you are teaching it is always important to have an agreed starting point. It is essential to start with what the students already know and not to assume anything. There are a whole host of Assessment for Learning strategies out there that you can use. One of the best ones to keep a constant check on the understanding of your classes is the traffic light system. You can use it in a number of ways but the basic principle is that green means you understand and are getting on with your work, yellow means you're not sure on some things and red means you feel a bit lost and aren't sure what to do. You could make signs for the students to hold up or have different coloured cups for them to place on their desks and change as they see fit. You could also use it as a way of target-setting; for example, by going over a number of topics and placing them in the pertinent coloured area. The traffic light system is adaptable and easy to use; once the students understand the concept you can apply it in various ways, even incorporating peer assessment into it. If you don't have time to prepare, another option is to simply use hands: holding up five fingers means 'I'm all over this' and none means 'What now?', with one, two, three and four for everything in-between.

C – Classroom practice

▪ Customer comment cards – I am sure you will have seen these at restaurants and shops, so why not use them in your classroom? It is a strategy that needs to be used well (you will certainly get a fair amount of garbage along the way) but with a bit work and commitment you might obtain some really useful information. Here are some ways to implement it:

- A feedback box keeps it informal and anonymous; on the downside it may be unproductive and produce a fair amount of rubbish (quite literally).
- You could give each student three personal cards or create a feedback section in the front of their workbooks. In this way it is personal to them and it gives you some form of tracking.
- Sticky notes can be stuck on the door when leaving the classroom.

I would strongly recommend discussion as a starting point – ask the group to come up with some appropriate and inappropriate examples to give them some initial guidance. Just like any other tool, they need to learn how to use it and make the most of it so it benefits them.

However, some words of warning: if you are going to use a feedback system be prepared to receive some abuse. My advice is try not to take it personally; if it's offensive then follow it up but if it's just done badly aim to take care of it in a low-key way and away from the whole class. The worst outcome is confrontation because the idea is to keep an open environment and an open mind. I would also recommend that you bring all the data together at some point and present it to the students – a tool like this is only any good if the results are there for everyone to see. What is most likely to get this kind of system working well is visible change which you then discuss as a group. I have found this strategy to be far from foolproof, and it takes guts to try it, so well done if you do and a huge well done if you actually get it to work!

- Mentoring – I have often found mentors to be helpful – someone who you know you can be completely honest with and who will help you out regardless of what mess you might be in. The most important factor is that it should be someone the student trusts and can talk to openly. One of my teachers used to meet me every lunchtime and go over my day with me; he would look through my books if he needed to and generally helped me to get myself organised. It was always reassuring to know that when things started to slip I had someone who had my back covered before things went completely down the toilet. If you employ this strategy in your school, try to ensure that mentor and mentoree meet on a regular basis and tailor the meetings around the student's difficulties. If the mentor is a member of staff then they can liaise with other staff members to find solutions to any problems that come up. There is also something to be said for peer mentoring and buddy schemes which some schools operate as part of a vertical tutor group. I wouldn't suggest relying on them completely but it can work well as part of an incorporated system of support.

■ The key to keywords – Many teachers have a keywords section in their classroom, perhaps on the wall or whiteboard. It is a great way to get subject-specific terminology across and can be advantageous for those students with dyslexia. There are a few things you can do to maximise their effectiveness: first and foremost is to make sure you use them. Refer to keywords on a regular basis and ensure they are used in a number of forms and in context. Use them yourself when you are talking and encourage your students to do so in their verbal and written answers. Try to emphasise and praise students when keywords are used well. If you can display them in more than one place even better; it may even be worth giving dyslexic students their own personal lists so they can refer to the correct spellings if needed.

B – Behaviour

■ Delayed punishment – When you think about the typical teenager you probably imagine a menacing mood-swing machine uttering the phrase 'That's so unfair!' at every given opportunity. The truth is there is a lot more to young people than this stereotype and they can behave wonderfully when given the opportunity. The problem is they can also be the menacing mood-swing machine when given the opportunity. Should the latter occur the best approach is to delay punishment to a later occasion; the principle being that everyone gets a chance to calm down, including you, and hopefully you can approach things a little more rationally. In this way you avoid creating a confrontation where things can easily escalate and get out of control. The teenage mind can be very volatile and when it comes to conflict the reptilian part of the brain readily becomes engaged and it can be hard to stop. You end up in a classic fight, flight, freeze or flock situation,[31] none of which are overly appealing. The student should realise they have done something wrong but you also inform them that you need some time to think about what you are going to do about it and that you will let them know your decision later. You can then take the opportunity to see them at breaktime or after class when you have a clear plan and can create a less hostile environment. They won't feel under pressure to act up in front of their peers and you might even find that the extra time they've had to think things through means that you can both get on the same page. After all, there is no point in punishing someone if they don't understand why they are being punished. If you have ever had a dog then you know what I mean!

■ 'And breathe' – Imagine what it might feel like if you had never felt anger before and suddenly you did: how would you even begin to describe it? Emotions are tricky things and life is full of them. It is hard enough sometimes when you know what's going on, but it is a lot harder when you are young and many of your feelings are new to you. It is easy to forget that your students aren't always sure what they are actually feeling because they are coming across new experiences, even if only small ones, on a regular basis. Often we learn these aspects of life simply through living – we learn to react appropriately to the things that happen to us. It would be impossible for me to teach you anything about a feeling without you having experienced it first; but what I can do is help you to understand and control your emotions. As teachers, this is something that we should really try to help our students achieve; understanding feelings and developing emotional intelligence is as important as maths or history, perhaps even more so.

When we relate this to dyslexia, often we are dealing with individuals who feel isolated, are lacking in confidence and self-esteem and find it particularly difficult to describe how they feel. This can create problems because not only are they more vulnerable to the stressors of school life but they find it hard to express themselves. It is always worth having a set of strategies for helping students to cope with stress and emotions, whether it is something you use with a whole class or on a one-to-one basis. A good technique to employ in the classroom is STAR (Stop, Think, Act, Review). It is a simple four-step process for students to follow which you can display on your classroom wall. You can also incorporate other simple techniques, such as breathing exercises and counting. For example, in the Stop phase you might talk to your students about taking a deep breath and counting to ten. This technique gives students a chance to consider their actions and then reflect upon them before acting, with the emphasis on consideration and learning. This system naturally follows the reflective learning process meaning that even if your students make a mistake you can loop it back round again until they get it right. You might even consider having areas of the classroom where students can take time out and have a chance to reflect or take a moment to themselves and count to ten. It's important to remind students of the tool and take the time to introduce and reinforce it. This may make a good PSHE lesson where you can use examples, e.g. what would they do if someone was trying to distract them? This is a strategy that you could choose to use with an individual who is having difficulty controlling their emotions or it might be something that you do with a whole class.

- The power of positive thinking – In 2011 Derren Brown had a series on Channel 4 called *The Secret of Luck*. The show looked at how the idea of luck affected behaviour and if this could be changed by making people believe they were lucky. What he found was that individuals who thought they were lucky had a much more positive approach to life and took far more opportunities. The fact that they thought they were lucky actually changed their behaviour and in a way made them luckier. The same applied for those who thought they were unlucky: they passed up opportunities even when they were right in front of them because they simply failed to look. So although the concept of luck is rather tenuous, the notion is self-perpetuating – we really do generate our own luck.

What does this have to do with teaching? Well, you could plant a lucky charm in your classroom and tell all your students that this will make them perform better in exams! Perhaps more apposite is the idea that your frame of mind can have a huge impact on the way you approach your life and hence your learning. Anything we can do to promote a sense of positivity, or even luck, is worth trying as it could have tangible results. You could link this to the affirmation process mentioned above, but it is also relevant to the small changes – for example, putting a positive spin on events. There is even research which shows that positive, optimistic people actually live healthier and longer lives than their pessimistic, negative counterparts.[32] So by creating an upbeat environment you could be performing a public health service! If this is something that really takes your interest then there are two avenues of pursuit I would highly recommend. Firstly, the Pacific Institute runs a variety of courses around their Investment in Excellence programme looking at affirmations and the power of forward thinking.[33] Secondly, if you are looking for further literature, psychologist Carol Dweck has done some very interesting research which appears in her book *Mindset*.[34]

■ DOH! – We all make mistakes, some of us more than others, but there are a few simple principles that we can use to help us out when we do. *Discipline* to help us stay on task and focus on what we need to do. *Optimism* to make sure that we have a positive approach to what we are doing. *Honesty* so that if we do make a mistake we can be truthful about it and work towards making it better. Discipline, Optimism and Honesty, or in the great words of Homer Simpson, 'DOH!' This little acronym is easy to remember and can be employed in a variety of ways. The idea behind it is simple and, because it isn't fixed to any particular situation, you can apply it no matter what. It is very important that your students have a good understanding of both the meaning, application and importance of each area, but once you have this established it can be an incredibly powerful tool. Use this principle to encourage pupils to take ownership of their behaviour and understand its importance; rather than telling them what they are doing wrong you can ask them!

With older students encourage them to come up with their own principles as a group. You can then display them on the classroom wall or in the front of their workbooks. You could even incorporate the principles into your reward schemes. This way everything remains very positive and, even when problems emerge, you have an immediate solution. For example, if Billy is talking over someone else, simply say 'DOH! What are you missing there Billy ... *discipline*?' Straightaway he knows that he has done something he shouldn't, he understands why and he also knows what he needs to work on to correct it.

Chapter 6
Technology

In an ideal world we would supply every child in every class-room with a top-of-the-range laptop or iPad, or both. But before you beat me over the head with your budget, that isn't what I'm suggesting. I have always been a huge fan of tech-nology – used in the right way it can be an incredibly powerful tool to maximise learning. Furthermore, the ability to use it is becoming an increasingly important skill in the workplace. Most of us wouldn't be able to get through our day without it. The fact of the matter is that technology is playing an ever more important role in the lives of our students and, as educators, we should be taking this into account; not teaching children for today's world but empowering them to solve the challenges of the future. Now before you march down to the head's office and demand the next generation of super-computers with 12-core processors (that's the power of 12 computers in one!) I suggest you look at the simple and effective things that you can do with a tight budget and what you have in front of you already.

For example, one of the best things I have ever learned to do is to touch-type; you don't need a particularly good computer to do it, just a PC with a word processor. As someone with dyslexia and dyspraxia, I find physically writing remarkably difficult and in fact hardly ever do it now. I can touch-type twice as fast as I can handwrite and the end result is not only legible but I can manipulate and edit it as much as I like. I regard this kind of skill as a requirement; dyslexic or not, it is something that your students will find incredibly useful in later life.

Preparation, preparation, preparation ...

When attempting a piece of work, especially one which requires a large amount of written text (such as this book for example), it helps me no end to have it well planned out before I start. Usually I don't stick to the plan, but the process allows me to get my thoughts down on paper and gives me a rough idea of what the structure might be. Although you can always scribble down some ideas on a piece of paper, writing, drawing and doodling whatever you want, there is also a whole load of technology out there that can help you. Often people with dyslexia have a mind that works really quickly and a hand that can't keep up. Technology packages can help with organisation, make planning easier and more interesting and ultimately enable you to produce better quality work.

Mind mapping and the creative process

Make a dent in the universe.

Steve Jobs

Sometimes coming up with a brilliant idea is difficult enough, but for people with dyslexia often the problem is not just thinking of good ideas but rather getting them down on paper with any kind of structure. The planning process plays a huge part in helping you to gain clarity and structure your ideas. It is said that everyone has a brilliant idea in them; it is just about how you go about getting it out. Picasso once famously remarked: 'Every act of creation starts with destruction'. But if you don't fancy having your classroom destroyed every time you're after a good idea, I have combined the process of mind mapping with James Webb Young's model for idea creation.

The mind is a complex and wonderful thing that has baffled and bemused scientists, philosophers, psychologists and anyone who has ever had a light bulb randomly appear over their head. It is no surprise then that the process of mind mapping is not a simple one – chiefly because it is an attempt at structuring thought, which often has no real structure. There are many techniques and strategies you can use in order to help yourself, mind mapping being just one of them, but I would recommend starting with the generation of ideas – the creative process.

A blank piece of paper is a frightening thing and, when it comes to mind mapping, that one central word can be enough to block out other useful ideas that might come to you if you were having a chat with a friend or relaxing in the bath, or both! I am indebted in this section to Phil Beadle's *Dancing about Architecture* and Webb Young's model of the process for the generation of ideas.[35]

1. **Collect the raw materials (aka information)**

   When your students are about to start a mind map, get them to soak up anything and everything you can. It can be complete textbook or an off-the-wall idea with no apparent relevance to the subject – but the more raw material they can get their hands on the better. If they only stick to the textbook and what's already been written and done before then they will have a hard time spitting out anything original. Scrap what you know and start afresh; everything is related somewhere along the line and sometimes the most obscure things are enough to produce a moment of genius. It is beneficial to allow students to think creatively and dynamically at this early stage – give them a wide range of resources in a variety of formats. If you can get some cross-curricular information from other subjects then great. It is important that you encourage students to keep tabs on themselves; cue Step 2.

2. **Digest the materials**

   Once the students have lots of materials then they can get their thoughts down. If they prefer mind mapping software then use it, if they prefer the freedom of pen and paper then stick with that, or combine the two. I have often found myself scribbling down ideas and drawings before I stick it all on my laptop and organise it. People with dyslexia typically don't have a good short-term memory, so keeping track of relevant and useful information is really important. This is a good habit to get your students into and a really useful set of information to have at your disposal.

3. **Don't think, do nothing**

   This part is crucial. As Rick Chin points out, often our biggest problem is getting in our own way.[36] You need to slow the whole process down, give the students plenty of time and don't restrict them to working at set times. Even when writing this book I've had many days when I've sat down and thought, 'Today is the day – I'm going to get loads done!', and stared at a blank screen for hours on end. Then there are days when I'm on the train, in lectures or at school when I think of something brilliant. Plant the seeds with the raw materials and then try to avoid forcing it, let it come naturally.

The problem is never usually the task itself but rather the thought process required to complete it. For example, if I asked you to fill an A4 page with the most interesting ideas you could – if you were a reasonably good typist it wouldn't take you long to fill a page with text. What takes the time is deciding what to write; if you gave yourself plenty of time to plan and come up with ideas you wouldn't have any problem with getting them down. I am by no means suggesting that the students should start work the second they get the task, but I am proposing that they begin thinking about it as soon as they get it, and then get on with other things.

Children with dyslexia often have a slow processing time, so will require extra time to process information and sometimes will need extended deadlines. Whether this means you give students additional time for homework or assessments or not, it is certainly something you need to take into consideration. It is also worth thinking about how you can apply this in lessons – you need to ensure students have enough time to understand the information. Teachers are often pushed for time so one of the best tactics is to return to topics at a later date once they have had a chance to deliberate on them subconsciously. This may be a good opportunity to set some homework, perhaps based around the mind maps they may have created.

4. **Wait for the 'ah ha!' moment**

This is often hard to do in a school environment; teachers have a restricted time to deliver the curriculum as it is, without waiting for everyone in the class to have a brilliant idea on the side. But we can still help ourselves and our students. Don't be afraid to think outside of the box: why not take your students for a walk? Not only might it give them a chance for their very own eureka moment to emerge but the fact that they are up and active will increase their heart rate, circulate more oxygen and engage different parts of their brain. Central to this is the approach you adopt: how can you expect your students to come up with original ideas if you, as the teacher, already know the answer you are looking for? Throw away the worksheets and textbooks every once in a while and just have a discussion – you never know what they might come up with. The trick is to keep an open mind and give things a gentle nudge now and then. It is helpful to take the students outside of their comfort zones when you get the chance, which will help to keep all of them that bit more engaged, including the ones with dyslexia.

Go for a walk, take a bath, stare out of the window, but be ready! A time will come when they think up a great idea and will be in no position to do anything about it. This is the moment when preparation comes into play – being in the right place at the right time doesn't work in this case. If you have a good idea you need to get it down anywhere you can, so help your students by encouraging them to carry a Dictaphone or notebook, to make a note on their mobile phone or leave themselves a voice mail (as long as school policy doesn't get in the way). Just make sure that they remember! Children with dyslexia aren't renowned for their great memories so they need to get into the habit of keeping tabs on themselves.

5. **Test the idea**

For me this means having a conversation, getting my idea out there, playing about with it, evaluating it and then trying to work out the best way to structure it. This is where the mind map comes in handy and where using a computer really comes into its own. This is all about finding what works best for your students, but to give you some ideas, I tend to order and number my ideas, for example:

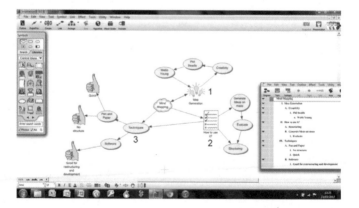

From here I can lay out my ideas, begin to make notes, fill in the gaps and gradually develop it into a finished product. The benefit of this approach is that you are constantly reviewing your ideas and building on them, and with the help of a bit of technology it is dead easy is to re-do things and mix them up if you need to. I have listed below some of the technologies I use and some others that are available. This process is something that you could do as a whole class, in small groups or individually. It is always good to have some form of collaboration if you can, and the whole-class method allows you to teach not just the subject but the process as well.

Inspiration

This is a simple but very effective piece of mind mapping software which I love. It allows you to simply click and type your ideas then link them together in whatever order you like. You can then go on to link files, change icons and add notes. The beauty of this software for me is in the ability to transition the mind map into an ordered plan which you can then transfer directly into Word. I would consider using this with a class, to present work or even to plan a lesson. There is even a free trial you can try so you can see if it works for you before you hand over any money. www.inspiration.com/

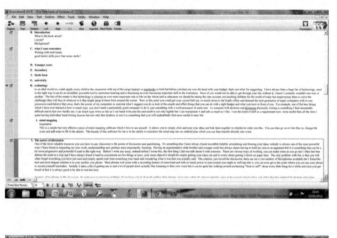

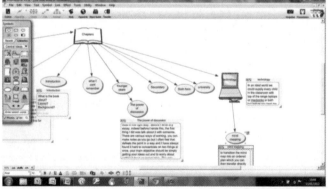

SpicyNodes

Far from some obscure kind of curry, SpicyNodes is web-based mind mapping software. It is similar to Inspiration in a lot of ways, but it is all done online in the cloud. The advantage is that you don't need to install anything and can use it in a variety of locations, as long as you have an internet connection. www.spicynodes.org/

MindNode

This is similar to SpicyNodes but with slight differences in styling; it is really a case of personal preference between the two. One advantage however is that MindNode is also available on touchscreen devices such as the iPad, if that is your preferred weapon of choice. http://mindnode.com/

Prezi

This isn't really mind mapping software per se as it has been built for delivering unique cloud-based presentations. This said, it can be used as one and is a great tool for teachers, and definitely makes a nice change from PowerPoint. Have a play with it and see what you think – there are a whole host of possible uses so be creative. http://prezi.com/

The brilliance of all of this software is that it allows the user to create order out of chaos, and it is mistake-free because it is so easy to rearrange and chop and change. That's really what makes this type of technology so good for people with dyslexia – you can get all your thoughts out quickly so you won't find your brain overtaking your physical capabilities, as might occur with pen and paper. Once you have got all your ideas down you then have a real chance to tackle the problem of structure as a discrete task. In this way it is possible get a very clear picture in your mind of what the completed piece of work might look like before tackling it head-on.

Stuff to help you read and write

The English language can be a wonderful thing – gloriously complicated and ever so slightly annoying; but far too often is it seen as the arch rival of dyslexia. However, if students can be equipped with the right tools then they may find themselves becoming good friends with the dictionary (or at least not want to find an elaborate plan to destroy it!).

Electronic readers

There are a number of programs to help you sift through that ever painful 30-page reading matter that everyone else seems to get through in five minutes. I use Texthelp Read&Write Gold. It is a good piece of software which can read Word documents, websites and PDFs out loud. This means you can use it to read pretty much anything, such as books or articles that you scan in. I find it particularly good for proof-reading my own work as well as going through lengthy texts. It works well because it highlights the word as it is spoken so you can read along at the same time. This allows students to take in the information through both sight and sound – a potentially powerful combination.

There are a range of settings so you can play around to tailor it to your personal preferences – everything from which voice is reading to you to the colour of highlighted words. It also provides a spell-checker which has been designed with dyslexia in mind. It not only comes up with a whole lot more spelling suggestions than you might normally get but it is also looks for particular mistakes frequently made by people with dyslexia. It has a facility to search for homophones which can be a particular problem. Plus it learns common mistakes that you as an individual might make which you can then add your own autocorrect function. In addition, you can add to the dictionary thereby enabling you to add words specific to your area; for example, I added a whole load of physiology words and teaching acronyms. You can even use the autocorrect as a slight cheat to add shortcuts, so you can type an acronym and get the full word to pop up in its place, making your typing experience even quicker. There is also a screen mask which can make tracking easier when you are reading or just make the screen a bit easier on the eye. Although electronic readers aren't foolproof, and can take a bit of getting used to, if you put in the initial effort your perseverance can really pay off. www.texthelp.com/

Writing

Your best friend has to be the keyboard: learn how to use it well and don't look back at that pesky pen. There are a number of free and paid-for touch-typing programs out there, some of which incorporate practice into games, but once you get your fingers in the right position it is just a case of programming in that muscle memory. If you can touch-type reasonably well you can type around 30–60+ words per minute, providing you can think them up!

Dragon NaturallySpeaking

Yes, I'm as disappointed as you – I don't mean a talking dragon. This is in fact a very clever piece of software which takes speech and turns it into writing. Although some people's experience of programs such as this can be quite negative, I would urge your students to try it out if they get a chance because the technology has come on leaps and bounds since it was initially produced. With a little bit of voice training and some practice it can work very well. It also comes with a voice reader, although in my view this is nowhere near as good as the dedicated electronic readers mentioned above. This software is not for everyone particularly if students struggle with speech as much as writing. However, if they have a block when it comes to writing then this could be right up their street. www.nuance.co.uk/

Dictaphone

Although strictly speaking a Dictaphone is not actually going to get the written word down on paper for you it does have a number of tricks up its sleeve. It is really easy to use and students may even have a simple version built into their phone. They can use it just to make verbal notes of a plan or even outline of what they want to say in a piece of written work before typing it up. On top of that it can be really useful for keeping notes when they are on the go or even recording important lectures or lessons. If they are like me – both forgetful and have a tendency to stare out the window when being told something important – then this can be a great help.

From a teacher's perspective, not only can you use a Dictaphone to make notes and so on but they can also be used to transform your lessons. There's no reason why you couldn't record particular sessions and make them available to the class. Being recorded can be a bit unnerving but on the other hand it may mean that you don't have to repeat yourself quite so often. You may even go as far as flipping your classroom completely. This teaching method involves delivering the content through video allowing you to have more one-on-one time on task in classroom. A really good example of this is through Khan Academy (check out their website: http://www.khanacademy.org) it has video resources which explain tonnes of topics. It really is worth a look and could save you time in the classroom. Your homework is your class content, and your class content is your homework.

There's an app for that

One of the most useful and powerful bits of technology I use is one that I carry absolutely everywhere – my smartphone. There is literally just about an app for everything and it is genuinely worth looking into how you can exploit this great resource. There is even an app that uses cartoons to help explain dyslexia!

iStudiez and iTeacher

The two apps that I find of most use are iStudiez and iTeacher. Essentially they are organisers designed around an educational lifestyle, whether that is school, college or university. iStudiez, for example, allows students to plan each term with different classes and assignments and then track their results. iTeacher follows a similar concept except it allows you to make a record of your students and track your classes down to results and attendance. The beauty behind these apps is that you can get them to work in conjunction with each other and track results and assignments. Overall they are great products and quite easy to use once you have taken the time to set them up.

Documents To Go

This app essentially allows you to access, edit and create files from your mobile phone. I can't say that I would rush to write anything substantial with it but it is worth having just to be able to access documents and make minor changes. With the addition of a Bluetooth keyboard, which you can connect to your phone, you can even write up notes and transfer them to your computer later. Not quite as good as a laptop (but a huge step up from a pen) but easier to carry.

Reminders

Reminders are already included on many smartphones. The brilliance of these is that you can set them to be time and location sensitive – for example, 'Hand in work when I get to school' – and ping!, you receive a reminder when you get there. Simple and effective.

Chapter 7
Exams and Qualifications

Educational testing and rating systems have been around for a very long time. Under the current GCSE system there is a split between examinations and coursework. However, the Secretary of State for Education Michael Gove has recently proposed a shift back to an exam-only system. This may have a damaging impact on dyslexic students for whom examinations can present a real problem. The very specific exam skills of reading and understanding a series of questions before producing a written answer – essentially a memory test within a set time limit – do not play to the strengths of those with learning difficulties. I am reluctant to say that exams are a useless test of a person but I do believe that they represent a very limited and restrictive snapshot, especially for someone with dyslexia.

The main problem is that exams focus on a number of tasks that dyslexics find particularly difficult. Reading and understanding the questions can present a fundamental problem, but there are also issues with working memory and processing speed. Add to this the need to formulate a written answer and add a timeframe to the mix, and you can have a recipe for disaster. But it is not all doom and gloom: there are strategies that can help.

The wider point is that we need to have a long hard look at what we are assessing and how we assess it – and try to be a bit more creative. There is a wider scope for this with vocational qualifications, such as BTECs, so this is something schools should consider when deciding which courses to run. However, with the continuing debate about the reform of the exam system this is one to watch. This chapter considers how best to use the qualifications currently available to the benefit of your students, along with some dyslexic-friendly techniques for exam success.

BTECs

Schools can run a wide variety of BTEC courses but these often receive very mixed views from both staff and students on their effectiveness. It is hard to knock the concept behind it, of a vocational qualification led by schools and tailored to students' needs. The syllabus is set centrally but the form of assessment is usually relatively open. In principle BTECs should work really well for students, especially those with dyslexia, as assessment can be adapted to their strengths.

Some schools pull this off brilliantly, but it is very easy to fall into the trap of setting lots of worksheets and essays. This is not the most effective approach and soon has students losing interest. I am not saying written work shouldn't play a part, but schools should try to be creative and offer as much variety as possible within each subject area. If there is any opportunity to use practical assessments then jump at it and think about applications for video and verbal appraisal where possible. If you are using a lot of written assessments, then make sure you offer clear guidance and ensure your students have been coached in how to plan and present good quality written work.

In Chapter 8 on higher education you will find some good techniques for planning work, but I would also recommend using structures such as PEEL:

- Point – Make a statement.
- Evidence – Back it up with evidence such as a reference.

- ▨ Explain – Describe how this reinforces your point.
- ▨ Link – Connect it back to the question.

For example: Is the PEEL method useful for students who have dyslexia?

- ▨ Point – The PEEL method is useful for students who have dyslexia ...
- ▨ Evidence – Because people with dyslexia benefit from having a clear structure to follow which is evidenced by my own experience and that 'Teaching should be structured, cumulative and multisensory, allowing time for the learner to see, say and do.'[37]
- ▨ Explain – Structure enables students to organise their thoughts and ensure that they cover all areas in a clear and concise manner.
- ▨ Link – PEEL provides this structure in the form of an easy-to-remember acronym which can be applied to written work, making it a valuable tool for students to use.

If you use methods like this be sure to provide subject-specific examples and perhaps even follow it up when marking by providing comments which relate to the method. Overall the principles behind BTECs are very sound but we need to ensure that as education providers we make the most of the vocational opportunities it offers us, rather than simply falling into altogether similar trap to the traditional exam system.

GCSEs

GCSEs currently take a range of forms and some subjects are more dyslexia-friendly than others. They form the staple diet of qualifications for most schools and constitute the measure of success for both students and schools. From my own conversations with teachers it seems that finding the right balance between getting students through their exams and actually teaching them can prove difficult. Sometimes as educators it is easy to get caught up in the cycle of meeting targets rather than teaching children; I dare say it is one of the dilemmas that many areas of the public sector face. Whilst qualifications are obviously important in life, they are not the be all and end all; more and more employers are saying that, at present, qualifications don't represent a well-rounded and successful individual but instead offer a rather limited perspective.

My advice to teachers is to try to teach subject content using a variety of methods. Those students with dyslexia will really benefit from practical and multisensory approaches and those without will probably find the diversity refreshing at the very least. When you come to set coursework be creative and offer variety – also take a look at the sections on mind mapping (p. 69) and creative writing (p. 105). If you can use a structured approach such as PEEL then that should also help. When it comes to examinations, students with dyslexia should at the minimum have extra time available to them and possibly with other support methods such as a word processor or 'reader'. The section below on exam technique, should give you a better idea of how to tackle the fiddly things in more detail.

Unfortunately, I can't in any way say what the future of the qualification system might look like with the potential to regress back to the two-tiered CSE and O level system of the past on the horizon. With Michael Gove, or any other politician for that matter, at the helm even my crystal ball isn't much help. Luckily we have managed to dodge the English Baccalaureate. I strongly believe that any solely exam focused system is a truly terrible idea, especially when it comes to students with dyslexia. Consider the two-tiered system of O levels, how do you decide into which group to put someone who may have dyslexia and although very bright in class lacks exam technique? Do you attempt to put them in the O level group and spend copious amounts of time teaching them exam technique? Or do you look for a qualification that is more suited to the individual and focus on developing their understanding and skills? It seems to me that the more you try and segregate qualifications the more you are going to get individuals stuck in the middle. If you are going to have two tiers why not have twenty? Or as many as you have students?

A levels

In a lot of ways, the A level has a number of similarities to the GCSE, it comes in a lot of different shapes and sizes and some fit people with dyslexia better than others. The key differences are that there is really a huge step up in the level of study and quite often an increase in the amount of independent study required. This is another one of those transitions that needs to be carefully managed and it's really important that if A level is the route your students are taking that they are as well informed as possible and make the right decisions as to which courses will suit them best. It's really important that they consider both the course content and how they are going to be assessed, they need to play to their strengths. Making that decision is something which I have gone into in a little more detail in the next chapter on higher education. Once on the A level road, as with a lot of higher education, I really think that time management becomes a big part of being successful. If exams are the assessment method then students need to consider how to manage the time available to revise and maximise their chances come the main event. Coursework presents a similar problem but students are working on the main event the whole time. It's a delicate balance for both and it is really worth spending some time on and making sure that you have measures in place to ensure that students don't get caught out with the last-minute scrambles to the finish line. A lot of the organisational techniques that I have mentioned earlier are going to help and by this stage hopefully students will begin to have developed their own preferred techniques. It's really worth having a bit of a game plan in place with your students with dyslexia, this is where having that neutral mentor in place can really help to avoid meltdowns. There are a lot of balls to juggle and a lot of it can be very new to your students. Check out the higher education chapter below for more help on organisation and writing techniques which should help. For exam technique take a look at the section further on in this chapter.

Exam v. coursework

As I mentioned before we could be looking at a big shift towards a more exam focused reform on the horizon, if Gove has anything to say about it that is. I don't however want you to think that when I say a completely exam focused system is bad that I mean coursework is the answer. As stated earlier, dyslexia is all about the individual, and it may so happen that one means of assessment better suits one person than another. Or even that perhaps one particular form of assessment suits one particular person in one particular subject at that particular level, if you see what I mean. We are going to be looking at pros and cons and likely end up with a nice big grey area somewhere in the middle. The point that I really want to get across is to make sure you have as many options as possible. I think sometimes we get confused when we talk about tailoring assessment to the pupil, it doesn't mean dumb it down and make it easy for them, it means make sure it's in a format they can access and that it does present a challenge.

When it comes to the particular downfalls of each for students with dyslexia you can be in a conundrum. On the one hand coursework tends to give you a lot more time, it gives you a chance to plan and discuss and work and re-work things but on the other hand it usually involves a large proportion of written work of some form or another. Exams have the solitude and time pressure and can often have a vast array of quick-fire and short answer questions. This is why it is important to have a balance and offer choice and support in whatever way we can. Unfortunately it seems that most of the time as teachers the choice of assessment is largely out of our hands, but should it ever present itself grab the opportunity and look for the option to give as much tailored assessment as possible and the biggest variety possible. I would say that if a course is only assessing in one way then it is only really finding out if you are good at one thing ... as opposed to a variety of skills applied to one subject. If the choice doesn't present itself and you are lumbered with exams then I would direct you to the section below for support and if the opposite then make sure you check out, the mind mapping section (p. 69) for planning and the section on creative writing (p. 105).

Exam technique

If you are a teacher or a student you have probably heard the phrase 'Make sure you read the question' at least a few thousand times. The fact is, however, that this isn't the most useful advice for someone with dyslexia. Nevertheless, good exam technique can make a huge difference to grades and it should be something that students are well-practised in. Each subject and exam will have its own specific areas to consider, but I have put together a list from which you can select the advice most appropriate to your students.

- Don't just read it, dissect it! – When you read an exam question it is vital to not just read it but to take it apart, especially when it comes to written questions. Underlining keywords is a good place to start and then reread the question. It is especially important to look to see if a question has a positive or negative slant to it. From here you can then begin to plan your answer.

- 'And that's a magic number!' – Look at how many marks a question carries to give you an idea of the length of the answer. For example a 3-mark question would be a relatively short answer question with three key points, whereas a 10-mark question requires a decent paragraph.

- 'I love it when a plan comes together!' – Take the time to write a plan to those long answer questions, even if it is just a quick set of bullet points. When I used to plan under pressure, I would jot down everything that came into my head in bullet form. I would then scrap anything I didn't like, group like things together and then number it off in terms of paragraphs.

- 'Extra, extra! Read all about it!' – When I was given extra time I often found that I managed to complete my work with some time to spare. Whether that is five minutes or half an hour, make sure you read through what you've done. You might remember something you had forgotten or spot a mistake you can correct.

■ Revision – I have used a number of crazy revision techniques but there may be some method in the madness. The usual revision cards and posters propped around the room always helped (I still have the equation for circular motion on my wall somewhere!). In terms of more adventurous techniques, I have heard of people listening to a particular album when studying a certain topic or eating a particular flavour sweet (or fruit if you want to promote healthy eating at the same time!). The idea is that you create an association in your mind and then repeat the activity just before the exam.

Another way to mentally prepare is to really familiarise yourself with exam papers and practise them as much as possible. I always started by simply working through them with my books next to me to refer to before moving on to attempt them in more exam-like conditions. This can really start to take the pressure out of exams and make them into a more everyday situation.

No stress, no mess

It is not that well known that people with dyslexia, and some other learning difficulties, can be very prone to stress, which often leads to their difficulties becoming more pronounced. This is another problem when it comes to examinations and testing as the increased pressure can easily lead to stress, which of course will only make things worse. Still, you don't want students to start stressing about stress otherwise it could end up in a vicious circle! However, this is a common problem for dyslexics, including myself.

As teachers we need to try to get the amount of pressure or challenge just right, and adapt our assessment methods accordingly. As bad as it sounds, stress isn't always bad; in certain ways it can push us to drive ourselves further than we normally would – and thereby achieve more. The difference can be both physiological and psychological; for example, stress causes a raised heart rate which in turn leads to better blood flow to the brain and increased brain function. Studies have shown that maze learning in rats increases in the short term when stress hormones are induced,[38] the point being that there is an optimal zone. Although it's also true that a rat's memory performance decreases under stress, something which perhaps we rely on more heavily as educators.[39] Finding this optimal zone is often mapped as challenge versus stress in an inverted U-shaped curve, the theory is learning increases with stress until a point when the stress becomes too great and performance begins to fall away. Although in the short term there are potential benefits to maintaining an optimal level of stress, it can be extremely damaging over the long term. There are a whole range of stress-related disorders which can occur – from fatigue to neural degeneration. When it comes to stress in the classroom we need to take extreme care: the right amount of pressure at the right time can produce excellent results. However, schools should aim to be largely stress-free zones for students (even if it isn't always for teachers!).

Although the science is sufficient to give us a broad under-standing of stress, unfortunately it isn't yet something we can simply apply to everyone. There is no one fixed point where everyone's learning is optimal; it varies with the individual. One person's stress could be another person's comfort zone. It comes down to your genetic make-up and your life experi-ence, both of which will have an impact on how well you cope with stress.

If we consider stress in terms of dyslexia, we know there is a genetic aspect to the condition plus there are likely to be similarities in the life experiences of sufferers, particularly within the education sector. To give this a little more context, if someone with dyslexia has a history of stressful experiences surrounding reading and writing, then just the idea of writ-ten work can be enough to promote a stress response. The prospect of an important exam coming up will induce even further anxiety for a student with dyslexia. The combined pressure of their weaknesses being assessed alongside the usual stressors can push them beyond coping point. Low self-esteem is also a problem with many dyslexic students having little or no confidence in their work. I have known people with dyslexia, myself included, to get extremely worked up just over the fact that someone will see their work.

It should also be remembered that if a high proportion of schoolwork involves reading and writing, which is something that causes students with dyslexia a great deal of stress any-way, then these individuals could be in a situation where they spend the majority of their school day in a heightened state of anxiety. This is not conducive to learning and may have damaging long-term effects. One of the biggest causes of stress in a school environment is deadlines, especially when a number of them clash and the sheer volume of work becomes overwhelming. This is when it is beneficial to have a mentor who can negotiate deadlines and help students to prioritise more effectively.

Teaching students how to understand and deal with their emotions is all too often missing from our packed school curriculum. However, it is something that as teachers we could be more proactive about – there are plenty of useful strategies to help manage these situations (see for example the 'And breathe' section on p. 61). Some of the warning signs to look out for include weight loss, tiredness, slight depression and becoming withdrawn.

The stress response is very easy to turn on but much harder to turn off, and as primates we are better at activating it than any other animal. As Professor Robert Sapolsky of Stanford School of Medicine observes:

Primates are super smart and organized just enough to devote their free time to being miserable to each other and stressing each other out ... But if you get chronically, psychosocially stressed, you're going to compromise your health. So, essentially, we've evolved to be smart enough to make ourselves sick.[40]

So if it makes you feel any better, when you do start feeling stressed it's only because you've evolved to be super smart – on that note you can relax!

Chapter 8
Higher Education

There are a range of qualifications out there from your traditional academic subjects right the way through to Harry Potter studies! Hopefully this chapter will help you find that little bit of magic to get your students through their higher level studies.

The most important factor when thinking about sixth form, college or university is choosing the right course, and there are a whole host of considerations your students should bear in mind. My advice on this subject is, *don't dive in* – young people need to make sure they are happy with their final decision. Where possible encourage them to try out different things, this could be in the form of work experience, taster days or even just talking to someone with first-hand experience. You can even get them to visualise themselves in those situations. They don't necessarily need to decide what they are going to do for the rest of their lives but they should make sure they pursue a subject they enjoy. If they are thinking about university they also need to weigh up the costs versus the gains, because if they aren't fully committed it probably isn't worth the £30,000-plus debt and three years of their lives.

To ensure this doesn't happen to your students, get them to take a moment, close their eyes and imagine sitting in a lecture or lesson with someone groaning away on their subject of choice. Then they should imagine working through piles of books and writing thousands of words on that topic. If they can still find their passion for the subject after this visualisation then they should jump right in and go for it. If not, then I am not saying they should give up on it but maybe they need to think things through more deeply and consider all the options.

Enjoyment is key because, when things get difficult, they will always find the drive and determination to get through to the other side. For all students, maintaining their motivation to stick with it and complete the work is essential, especially for those who might struggle to remain focused at the best of times. For those students with dyslexia, it is likely that they might not engage well with every element of a degree course – particularly those with heavily written elements – so it is all the more important that they have that bit of extra drive.

How to organise your life?

There are a series of challenges to Key Stage 5 and university life, and that's before you even think about attending your first lecture/lesson or handing in your first assignments. For most students it is probably the first time they have had so much independence and this in itself presents a real challenge, especially if you already struggle to be organised. There are a whole host of balls to juggle from cooking, cleaning and finances through to working independently. There is definitely a technique to finding the right balance and hopefully the tips below might give your students a helping hand.

Money, money, money

One of the most significant changes to their lifestyle will probably be the need to manage their own income, so use those tutor times – or any opportunity you get to work with numbers – to get some useful advice across. It is very simple stuff but it comes more naturally to some than others. Those with dyslexia will benefit from having structures and techniques in place to manage their lives, both inside and outside of education.

■ Show me the money! – Make sure they know how much money they have to play with and where they are getting it from; then they need to budget.

■ Where the hell did all the money go? – Students should know their projected income and outgoings – what the costs are, how much are they and when they are due. General ones to think about are rent, utility bills and food, with booze and going out coming a bit lower down the list! You can always link this with some sort of business exercise.

■ Budgeting – Students may not think its fun but believe me it is necessary, as I have seen people go through their entire loan in fresher's week, as you may well know! Use plenty of real-life examples that are relevant to them and get your students to practise. It is surprisingly easy to get their attention when you start to put cash into the picture. If you are a maths teacher struggling to engage some of your pupils then ask them if they want to have a mortgage one day. Or perhaps get them to imagine they are at university and have a student loan (plus any additional income from part-time jobs or their parents), then give them different options of places to live, and ask them how they would budget accordingly. Give them a process to follow, such as allocating money for rent, food, bills, travel and other essentials. Whatever is left over can be put towards having a good time! Alternatively you could get them to budget for a night out – anything that might grab their attention. You can even use your own experience or your own time as a student as an example, anything to get them interested. This sort of practice might help them to make more informed decisions when it comes to the real deal.

- Jobs – Many of your students will be reaching the age when they can start to work and earn a bit of extra cash. If they can avoid having a job whilst at school, college or university then great, as they can focus more on their studies. If they can get a job during the holidays even better. However, if they do need to work during term time then try to persuade them not to overdo it and help them to make considered decisions where possible. It is all about time management: encourage them to carefully consider how to use their time most effectively.

■ Food for thought – This may sound silly but I have always been terrible at organising food. I love cooking and I'm not bad at it, but I often find myself in a rush and skipping meals. It makes a huge difference to our health and energy levels if we don't eat properly – even missing just one meal. You might soon stop feeling hungry but perhaps you'll get tired and stressed – and it is easy for things to snowball. I know of one teacher who had a particularly troublesome group and so one day brought in a whole load of hot-cross buns for them to eat at the start of the lesson. He soon found that they settled down nicely. I am not suggesting that you feed your students every lesson, but it might be a helpful way to explain the importance of a well-balanced diet.

Time management

I would be lying if I said I'd never missed a lecture because I was completely exhausted and massively overslept. It is easy to make simple mistakes – maybe you're not sure where you're going, how to get there or you leave a little late. The point is it always pays to be prepared, so make sure your students have the tools and skills at their disposal to use their time wisely. For many students it is the first time that they've had free periods and a choice about how to use their time, but often they need guidance in order to make the right decisions. Many of them will waste their time and make mistakes, but as long as they learn from any slip-ups then this will be of great use to them when it comes to entering university or the workplace.

If you are mentoring a student with dyslexia, as soon as they've got their timetable go through it with them and print off a couple of copies – at least one to carry and one for the bedroom wall. Even better than carrying a paper copy is to transfer it onto their phone, either using an existing calendar or a specific timetable app such as iStudiez (see p. 82). Encourage them to make clear choices about how they are going to use their spare time between lessons and outside of school. You don't want to tell them what to do, but it is helpful to ask the right questions and check they are thinking their decisions through in advance.

Making writing exciting

Almost all degree courses contain a significant amount of assessed written work, and a well-written essay or exam answer can make a huge difference to final grades. Sometimes writing can seem like a laborious task – and if it seems boring to write it then it will probably be boring to read! Here are a few rules that I have always tried to follow to keep things interesting and hopefully score higher marks along the way.

- Planning – It is so important for students have an idea of what they want to say before they try to put it on paper. When you start to get into longer length essays it is incredibly easy to lack structure and lose your way, so plan! (Take another look at the mind mapping section on p. 69). They don't need to stick rigidly to the plan but it will definitely help to give them an idea of what

105

they want to say. This is something you might want to practise in whole-class or small group discussions – each group forming an essay plan and then presenting it to the class. It can be a really effective way of getting practice quickly without having to write the essay every time.

▨ Write like you're telling a story – By this I don't mean start essays with 'Once upon a time ...' (although that would be fun!); rather make sure that written work has a coherent structure with a clear beginning, middle and end.

▨ If you say it then back it up – When students arrive at university they will be bludgeoned with the concept of referencing and how to do it properly. This is something that would be really beneficial to introduce to them during school. It doesn't need to have quite the same rigorous structure as required at university level, but simply stress the need to back up their points. Students will be much better off rewriting a quote in their own words, unless it is particularly good, but they should still think about providing the source. Plagiarism is a hot topic for a lot of universities and carries series consequences, many universities are now using computerised checking systems, so it's really important that students get into good habits. It is a good idea to get them used to the idea of picking out relevant information and constructing an answer from it. This could be done in groups – everyone researching a topic together, sharing their sources, picking out the relevant pieces of information and presenting this to the whole class. Children with dyslexia will find it difficult to read through reams of text so help them by teaching them how to find the information they need (see the section on research on p. 114) and encourage them to use a variety of sources.

■ Be controversial – If your students really want to get those higher grades then they need to be a little bit different. It is very important that they reference their work and have a strong understanding of the material, but if they really want to lift their work up a level then they need to find an edge. The approach required will vary hugely depending on the subject but persuade students to think outside the box and explore a number of avenues before drawing their conclusions. A good place to start is with research that is not necessarily directly related to the subject in question but could have a potential connection which may have been overlooked before. For example, I once used an article from the *New Scientist* about the nature of free will and related it to the social structure of sport. Grab whatever resources you can and give your students examples of how they might try to be different. Those verbally intelligent students with dyslexia will probably grab this idea and run with it – just try to spark their interest.

■ Start early – The road to hell is paved with good intentions, as they say, and I have watched as my good intentions left me poring over my laptop until 3 a.m. trying to finish the essay which was due the next day. If your students can learn from my mistakes (or yours) then brilliant; if they need to make their own then get them out the way now! Even if you can only get them to plan well in advance it is worth doing. You don't want to be constantly chasing students for work so you need to set a clear target and have them hold themselves accountable. The more you use words like 'have to' or 'must' the more their work is going to become a chore. Get your students to become self-motivating – most of them will want to do well (even the ones who don't seem to) and if you can translate that into them making a conscious choice to work hard, then great. If they end up at university handing in work late, even by five minutes, this can lead to a deduction in marks and result in overall lower grades. No one makes that mistake more than once. This doesn't mean not offering any second chances, but it does help to establish structured consequences. It may take them a while to come around, but perseverance is key.

▪ Rework and remould – Once students have completed their work encourage them to reread it and not to be afraid to mix it up and change it. Then they should ask somebody else to go through it for them, then go through it again themselves, then go through it with someone else, then read someone else's work and then their own again. Only then should they hand it in. This is well worth doing – they can't be expected to get it perfect first time, even if they need to make only very minor changes. Introducing self- and peer-assessment techniques can also save you from having to mark everything a million times. Don't forget, however, that these techniques will need to be taught – don't expect to get good constructive feedback from the students without some coaching.

Help, I need somebody, and not just anybody!

The support available for students in higher education with learning difficulties is exceptionally good, especially at university level, and is usually well-tailored to the individual and the course. It may help your students to have some information about what is available in advance, where applicable. If students or parents come to you looking for help, here is how to point them in the right direction and alleviate some of their worries.

If the student is lucky enough to have already been diagnosed with dyslexia then the best approach is to contact the institution as early as possible and get the ball rolling. Universities often have a department dedicated to dealing with learning and other disabilities and will usually ask for copies of any previous assessments from the school or elsewhere to be sent to them. Typically students will then be sent to the nearest available test centre to the university where an independent report can be done. This generally evaluates several measures including verbal and written IQ as well as a reading age. It could sometimes be the case, as it was with me, that a student's reading and writing ability is average or just below average, but they perform much higher verbally.

Students may also find themselves with a preliminary diagnosis of another learning disability. For example, I was told that I had tendencies associated with dyspraxia (which I already knew) and attention deficit disorder. These can then always be followed up if necessary. A full report will be written up and sent to the university so they can proceed to a needs assessment, during which the student will talk to an adviser about the resources and options available and any relevant suggestions. This can be anything from technical equipment such as laptops, printers and software through to weekly meetings with an adviser. The final needs assessment report will recommend the required level of support and include a number of costings from a range of companies who can provide the equipment required, from which the student should select the one that is most acceptable. Then it is simply a case of waiting for the student finance department to pay for the equipment and put the order in, before the suppliers can contact the student with regards to delivery and any training sessions which may be required. From my experience this usually involves the trainer from the company in question coming to wherever you wish to have the training. Once the training is complete then you're off, and you should only need to contact the providers if there is a problem.

If that all seems a little long-winded then that's because it can be! It took me the better part of a year to get through the process, so it is really worth making sure students are in the know and get it underway as early as possible. If things get off to a good start then it could take around four months. If you want your students to really get a head start then badger them to call the university and apply for Disabled Students' Allowance (DSA).[41] It can help to speed up the process if there is as much evidence of support as possible and background information from the school, so be sure to pass on what you can.

If students are yet to be diagnosed as dyslexic, but are suspicious or just plain curious, then again they will need to contact the university or education provider. They should be offered a preliminary test and an informal meeting. If the institution feels that the student does show dyslexic tendencies then the university will ask for them to be formally tested (following the same process as outlined above).

Course leaders and teachers/lecturers should be notified when they have a dyslexic student and often a dyslexia-differentiated marking system will be put in place, usually in the form of a sticker handed in on your work. If this isn't something you already do at your school it is really worth considering – a gentle reminder to staff not to scrawl red pen over every single spelling mistake can do a lot to stop students feeling persecuted. At university I was lucky enough to have a head of course who took an interest in me from the start of my course and offered help me out; it can make a real difference.

Now is also a really good time for students to begin to take ownership of their own condition – so whether they are a little unsure about something or having a 'class A' breakdown, they have someone to talk to who can either help them directly or point them in the right direction. Again, it can be helpful to have a network of support in place, including friends, teachers, support staff and parents, with the student at the centre and in control. When a problem occurs often the solution is very simple: if you are mentoring a student, or just there to offer a helping hand, make sure they know that the worst problems are usually easily fixed and there is no shame in getting the help they need and deserve.

Higher education is one of the stages of education where excellent help is generally available – but it is up to the student to seek it out and make the most of it. Whether it is school, college or university, there will come a point when there is no one to intervene on their behalf any longer. It isn't about parents evenings any more, it's students evenings! So now is your chance to empower your students – make sure they know the phrase 'If it's to be, it's up to me!'

The boredom of lectures

I have been in my fair share of interesting lectures and dull ones. Apparently no one sees the irony of having a boring lecture on the importance of making lessons interesting. The fact is the idea behind lectures *is* boring, even the word 'lecture' is boring! The notion of someone talking at you for hours on end about something, which I am sure at one stage was brilliantly interesting, but very quickly turns into a dull background drone while you clock-watch just doesn't work for me and I am sure a lot of others. Although it may not be a completely useless concept, we know that the more engaged a student is the more they are likely to learn, and perhaps a lecture is not the most engaging spectacle. The idea that people simply absorb knowledge just because someone very clever verbalises it is a false one. Attention span is shown to be from anywhere between 5 and 40 minutes depending on the task in question.[42] People aren't designed to focus for long periods of time unless they are intrinsically well-motivated to do so or have regular breaks to recapture their attention. That goes for both you and your students. Your students are now becoming adults; perhaps they may need to act like it more often, but even adults aren't happy to just sit still and listen.

As a teacher you need to find ways to make your lessons (or lectures) captivating. It doesn't need to be all singing, all dancing, but a good lesson needs to make students think and ask questions. Even better would be to get them actively involved in an activity. The best lectures and lessons I have had are the ones that caught me off guard and involved a novel experience which remained in my mind. For instance, the lecture I had on morals and ethics which looked at whether helping someone was morally right if you didn't have pure intentions when doing so. The example used in this case was a man helping a young woman change a car tyre on the off-chance of receiving a sexual favour! It may have been crude but it worked; it got people talking and it stuck in their memories. I am not suggesting that you relate all your lessons to sex, although it probably isn't a bad place to start with a bunch of late adolescents.

To make a session interesting try breaking it down into bite-size chunks, which are split up with some form of active engagement, and endeavour to include some form of unusual experience. If you can build in an opportunity for a practical task, or even just randomly moving seats, it may keep your sleepy students from passing out at the back. The point is: do whatever you have to do to make them sit up and take notice, and once you have their attention don't let it go! PowerPoints are usually exhausted within the first week of term, so mix things up and don't let students fall into too much of a pattern. Now is a really good chance to get them out of their comfort zones on a regular basis.

Research

Trawling through books can be exceedingly boring, especially when it can take twice as long to read, as is often the case if you have dyslexia, and all you are really looking for is one key sentence. However, research is one of the most important aspects of higher education study so it is really worth putting in some time and effort into teaching your students some of the tricks of the trade. It can also be valuable if they share their resources – as long as it is not one-sided and they aren't writing one another's essays – so try to encourage collaboration.

E-mazing!

Dyslexic students should jump at any access to electronic versions of books or journals. They can be much easier to use – primarily because you can hit Ctrl-F (or Find and Replace) and type in any keywords that relate to what you're after and *bam!* – instant results, much quicker than actually reading through the whole volume.

Here are some other resources to share with your students;

- Google Books – Usually my first port of call as there is a good selection and it is very easy to use. Try a few different searches to see what you can find. http://books. google.com/

- Google Scholar – Much like its book-related counterpart, Google Scholar is very similar except it searches for journals and academic papers. http://scholar.google.com/

- University/school/college library – Your respective establishment might have its own electronic library or access to a paid-for e-journal site.

- National, Academic and Specialist Library Catalogue – A brilliant website for accessing journals and articles, most of which are free or give you a substantial preview. It has a good range of search parameters and lots of resources over a wide range of subjects. http://copac.ac. uk/

- eBooks.com – Although this not a free resource it does offer gratis previews and you can unlock full copies for a cost. So if you think that there is something worth owning then this is a good place to look, especially if like me you prefer your books in megabytes as opposed to ink and paper. http://ebooks.com

- Wikipedia – You might think this is a silly suggestion but Wikipedia can be a great source of information – you can search for specific topics and get detailed overviews. Everything is generally well-referenced and monitored. The trick is not to reference Wikipedia itself but instead to check out the references cited and explore them further. http://en.wikipedia.org/

- Google Play – This is another e-book store. If you need to make a purchase it is certainly worth a look, plus the files are compatible with PCs, Macs, phones, tablets and e-readers, meaning you can access them from a number of locations. There is often a link from Google Books if the e-book is available to purchase. http://play.google.com/

- iBooks textbooks for iPad – Apple has recently set about trying to revolutionise another area of life – the textbook. Apple has made a special tool available to publishers to develop their own specialised textbooks specifically to take advantage of the iPad's extensive features. If you already have an iPad this could work out cheaper in the long run. Currently the retail price of e-textbooks is markedly cheaper than their physical counterparts and it may be that in the long term it could be a better investment for a school or department. The textbooks themselves have all the benefits of an e-book but with additional interactive features. It is certainly an option worth looking into; even if it might not be viable currently, I would put money on it being the future of textbooks.

Students with dyslexia might find these research methods are far easier to use than the more traditional routes – just make sure you take the time to teach them how to use them correctly. One program which also complements this method of research is Google Chrome; not only do I consider it the best web browser but there are a number of extensions which can be very useful. Session Buddy is a very effective tool, as it enables you to save web sessions and open them again at a later date. This means you can keep all of your precious research pages in one safe place and know that you won't lose it when it comes to writing up a bibliography.

The old-fashioned way

There is still something to be said for the more traditional methods of doing things, but there are some simple steps to make this easier for students with dyslexia. Using a library can be really hard at first, but there are a couple of tips. Many libraries now have an electronic catalogue which is definitely worth using. Better still, most university libraries have subject specialists and librarians who can point students in the right direction. After that, it is all about making sure that students use the books effectively. Some course books are worth reading from cover to cover but often you are just looking for one particular section. Formulate a process that students can follow to find what they are looking for; for example, ensure they know how to use the contents, glossary and index to best advantage. I would also advise using sticky notes to keep track of important points.

Chapter 9
Teaching

I would like to start this chapter by observing that there is a good chance that you have been reading this book and wondering if you might be in that 10% of the population affected by dyslexia and whether it could be worth taking a test yourself. If you think this might be you it is worth checking out the checklist on the British Dyslexia Association website.[43] If you are reading this as the parent of a child with dyslexia I would also recommend you take a look, as there is a chance you may have dyslexic tendencies yourself.

When it comes to teaching with dyslexia my experience so far is limited. During my teacher training there was no real focus or particular taught area on dyslexia, although it was occasionally mentioned. Although this is not so surprising in PE, it was mentioned during classroom teaching elements as part of a differentiation approach. This often led to some of my fellow teaching students listing it under a 'less able' approach, much to my amazement. There were some indicated strategies but most of us would have benefited from more direct input about learning difficulties. I imagine this varies depending on where you study, but the good news from teacher training is that many student teachers are aware of dyslexia and have an idea of what the condition involves, even if it is not as broad as it could be.

As a teacher I adopt many of the strategies suggested throughout this book to overcome the problems I experience because of my own dyslexia. I use technology as much as possible and try to stay on top when it comes to organisation. But teaching isn't easy and at first glance having dyslexia could seem like a huge disadvantage. However, this depends on how you teach; everyone has their own style and it is important that you play to your personal strengths. It is all about finding your own form.

The key is to consider what you really want to achieve in each lesson before you start thinking about what you are going to do. For example, I might be looking at passing in football, but what do I *really* want those children to learn? Is there any value in me actually teaching them how to pass a ball? There might be some neuro-motor benefits or maybe some fitness gains. But if that is all I'm trying to teach them, then why not simply have them pass the ball to each other over and over and then run around the field several times? It would be better if I could get them to work as a team, or to be creative within a space or using their bodies at the same time. Now, that might seem a little too easy – after all, I love sport – but you can apply similar rules to any subject.

For example, I could be teaching about Henry VIII in history, but the pupils aren't likely to learn much by simply fixating on dates and learning that he wasn't a great husband. Instead I might want my pupils to be able to analyse a source and be objective about it. (For instance, if we found a source which stated that Henry's excuse for executing Anne Boleyn was because she snored, we might need to consider the veracity of our source!) Perhaps I could ask the students to think about the impact of religion on how a country is ruled or vice versa. Even better might be teaching the concept of evaluating information and collecting data to form a conclusion. Teaching students how to find value in a source and looking at what makes it valid requires a whole host of critical thinking skills. The point is: know what you want your pupils to gain from a lesson and make sure it is worth learning (and not just because someone decided it should be in the syllabus). Once you have identified the learning objective, then you can decide the best way for you to approach the problem. Your subject is a platform from which students learn a range of other skills.

Once you have decided what you want the students to learn, it is usually a case of making it into a formal learning objective which you then slap on a whiteboard. Personally I hate using whiteboards; as useful as they can be, they make me feel self-conscious (due to my rather poor handwriting) and I don't think it actually adds much to the lesson. Although learning objectives can be useful I don't think you always need one. Maybe the children would be better off writing their own learning objective or perhaps the class could discuss what they think the learning objective should be. At the end of the lesson they could discuss whether it matched what they actually learnt, and what else they learnt that maybe they didn't think about at the beginning of the lesson. There is more than one way to approach a problem; who knows, it might work out better in the end. It also could be a disaster, but as long as you learnt something from it, it was a worthwhile experience.

Create a sensation with classroom organisation!

One of the most difficult things I find about teaching with dyslexia is organisation. I find it hard enough to organise myself so when you add 30 students to the situation it doesn't get any easier. Organisational problems can create all sorts of trouble and before you know it your whole lesson has snowballed out of control. Having a comprehensible structure to your lesson will not only help you, but it will also assist your dyslexic students. If they are presented with a clear structure that they understand then they will be able to work within that space – think of it like setting the boundaries of a football pitch and then letting your students get creative in that space. This applies not only to the tasks and lesson progression but also just to the way you run your classroom: simple behaviour guidelines and clear expectations of what your students can and will achieve. There are a few strategies that I like to use as a dyslexic teacher that will hopefully help all the students in your class, but will sit particularly well with dyslexic students.

This is all about minimising stress and making life easier for you as well as your students. The best resource available to you in any classroom is the pupils themselves. If you can implement a system in which the pupils cover most of the organisation, half of the work is done for you! Ideally you want to create a structured system with set roles so that you don't have to go over it in every single lesson and waste time. Here's an example.

The Apprentice – classroom style
(just add Alan Sugar!)

This could work as a whole class or potentially even better in small groups, which adds a slight competitive edge. Simply create a series of roles, each with their own responsibilities, which you give out to each student, with the roles rotating through the group over your choice of timeframe.

- Project manager: Leader of tasks and in charge of delegation.
- Resource manager: Checks everyone has the right equipment that they need.
- Team Motivator: Keeps up team morale and makes sure everyone stays on task and happy. Could also be in charge of a reward system.
- Accountant: Keeps track of rewards for individuals and team.
- Coach/Mentor: Can act as an assessor for the group, giving points for good work and for improvement.

You need to make sure that these roles are clearly understood – you can't just leave it up to the students. As with anything else, they will need to learn how to use it properly so take the time to introduce it thoroughly and then use it consistently over a period of time. Ensure you give pupils a chance to get used to their roles before you switch them about. You could even introduce awards like 'project manager of the year' and so on or maybe someone gets 'hired' at the end of it all! It doesn't have to follow this exact system but the key is to keep it simple and then develop it further. Giving students responsibility for their own learning should not only help you as a teacher but will benefit your students' learning as well. The reason I like the 'apprentice' idea is because it relates to real life. Students have to work as a team and they understand the importance of working together in specific roles. It develops leadership, social and interpersonal skills. This technique can adapted and used at any age range.

Planning

Planning is essential to teaching but it doesn't have to follow a strict regime – everything from simply giving it a little thought and maybe jotting down a few notes to really detailed plans can work at different times. Once again, it is about finding out what is right for you. My experience of using a university planning sheet in detail for every lesson fell short for me sometimes. Detailed plans work well as long as everything is going to plan, but the problem was that when I needed to adapt to changed circumstances my plan could no longer deliver. Although I often tried to have a plan B up my sleeve, I couldn't help but feel that my lessons had a rigid structure and lacked flow. My solution was to pioneer a new form of planning – flow planning.

The aim is to plan but in a flow chart form, which I find to be quicker and more dynamic. Start with what you want the students to learn in the lesson: what do you want them to get out of it? Keep this simple and to the point and don't get bogged down in the details – you can flesh out the bare bones later. Just rattle off potential ideas and directions which should start to give you your potential structure. From there you can begin to refine things a little and begin to add some detail.

In the Appendix there is an example to give you a better idea of how a planning flow chart might look. Of course, you could go off on some completely different trajectories if you want to cultivate more options and add elements of choice for your students. You can also add notes to each area, including extra details such as set groups, any equipment you might need or links to resources.

One teacher or 30 classroom coaches?

It is common knowledge that we often learn best when we can teach something to someone else. This technique really maximises the work that your students can do to support their own and each other's learning. For example, a class could work in groups on different aspects of a topic, such as the principles of attacking play in team games or different characters in a play. They could then produce resources and plan to teach what they have learnt to other groups. Get them to tell you how they learnt best and how they would want to approach the next unit of work given the content and areas that need to be covered. Think of your class as one big team!

Keep learning active

Follow the 80:20 rule – 80% student participation and active learning and 20% teacher led. You want the children to feel they are tired because they have worked hard, not for you as a teacher to be exhausted because you feel as if you have done all the work! Get the students active on quick tasks as soon as they arrive in your class. Set your expectations high and they will work up to them.

Celebrate success

One final note, make sure you don't put a cap on your students or ever limit what they are capable of especially if they are dyslexic. Whenever you get the chance to celebrate their success do, make sure students with dyslexia know that they can achieve not in spite of their dyslexia but also because of it. If they need some inspiration here are just a few of the achievements by people with dyslexia:

Sir Richard Branson – Knighted entrepreneur and owner of Virgin with an estimated worth of over £3 billion. He not only built the business from the ground up, but he did it twice having been declared bankrupt!

Winston Churchill – One of the country's most renowned politicians who not only has some fantastic quotes but led the country through the Second World War. My two favourite quotes are: 'Success is not final, failure is not fatal: it is the courage to continue that counts.' And the second which you may recall from Stephen Fry on QI, was when Churchill was informed of the scandal of a backbench MP being caught fraternising with a guardsman in the bushes of St James Park. Churchill's response was 'very cold last night' and upon being informed that it was the coldest night of the year, he replied 'makes you proud to be British'. One of those quotes probably has a place on a classroom wall but I will let you decided which!

Jamie Oliver OBE – Reformed your school dinners, a superstar TV chef and world known brand. He owns over 16 restaurants and is estimated to be worth in excess of £150 million. Oh and he makes a pukka steak, Guinness and Cheddar pie!

Jørn Utzon – The architect behind the Sydney Opera House, which when it was recognised as a World Herritage site in 2007 was only the second person to ever have received such an honour in his lifetime!

Muhammad Ali – Famously wrote the poem 'I am the Greatest!' and went on to become arguably the greatest boxer of all time and one of the greatest sports people. One of the first people to actively use sports psychology to great effect, he played a key role in the US human rights movement. More recently he took part in the 2012 Olympic opening ceremony to recognise his achievements.

Will Smith – Aka The Fresh Prince has dominated a large part of the entertainment industry. He has had success as an actor in film and television, a director, producer and rapper. Just to prove that he is good at all those things he has four Golden Globe Awards, two Academy Awards and four Grammys to his name!

Henry Ford – Pioneer of the automobile, which most of us couldn't live without. His famous Ford Model T was named as such because 'T' was the only difference between can and can't. His best classroom wall quote would have to be; 'If you think you can do a thing or think you can't do a thing, you're right.'

Quentin Tarrantino – Perhaps the least of his achievements is that he is my favourite director but on top of that he is widely considered as groundbreaker in the world of cinema. He has received a number of awards including an Academy Award, a Golden Globe Award, a BAFTA and the Palme d'Or and has been nominated for an Emmy and Grammy.

Bill Gates – Founder of Microsoft one of the biggest technology companies in the world, and quite simply one of the biggest companies full stop. The aim to put a computer in every household in the world probably isn't that far off.

John Lennon – Arguably one of the most iconic musicians of all time. As a member of the Beatles he had seen huge success and even had solo success as well. He is responsible for 25 US number one singles and as a member of the Beatles enjoyed 69 weeks at the top of the charts. He has been inducted into the Singer Songwriter Hall of Fame and the Rock and Roll Hall of Fame. *Rolling Stones* magazine rated him as the fifth greatest singer of all time. He undoubtedly had a huge impact on music and culture around the world.

Joe Beech – Perhaps not quite among the greats yet but he did finally finish *The Little Book Of Dyslexia* and well, we will see about the rest …

Why not see if any of your students could add to this list!

I'd like to leave you with a couple of my favourite facts, courtesy of the *QI book of 1227 facts to blow your socks off*, which I think nicely summarise how you should approach dyslexia (best read in a Stephan Fry summing up voice):

More than 50% of NASA employees are dyslexic, hired for their superior problem-solving and spatial awareness skills.

and

The national research centre for Dyslexia is in Reading.

In other words, never underestimate someone with dyslexia, in fact you may be better of treating them like they have a superpower and make sure you have a laugh along the way.

Appendix

Planning flow chart (p. 126)

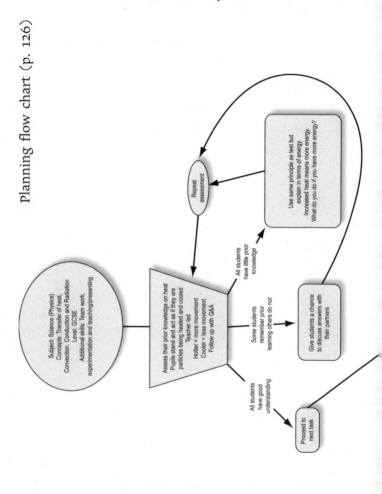

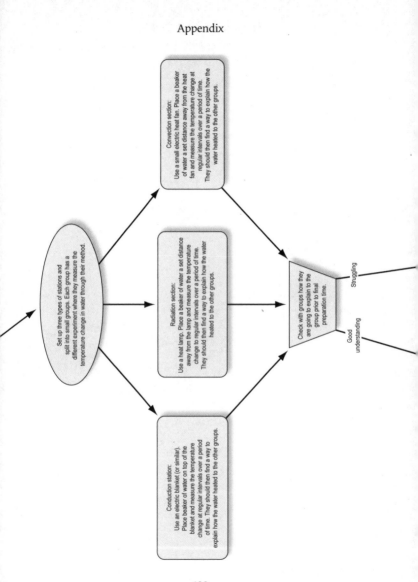

Set up three types of stations and split into small groups. Each group has a different experiment where they measure the temperature change in water through their method.

Conduction station:
Use an electric blanket (or similar). Place beaker of water on top of the blanket and measure the temperature change at regular intervals over a period of time. They should then find a way to explain how the water heated to the other groups.

Radiation section:
Use a heat lamp. Place a beaker of water a set distance away from the lamp and measure the temperature change at regular intervals over a period of time. They should then find a way to explain how the water heated to the other groups.

Convection section:
Use a small electric heat fan. Place a beaker of water a set distance away from the heat fan and measure the temperature change at regular intervals over a period of time. They should then find a way to explain how the water heated to the other groups.

Check with groups how they are going to explain to the group prior to final preparation time.

Good understanding

Struggling

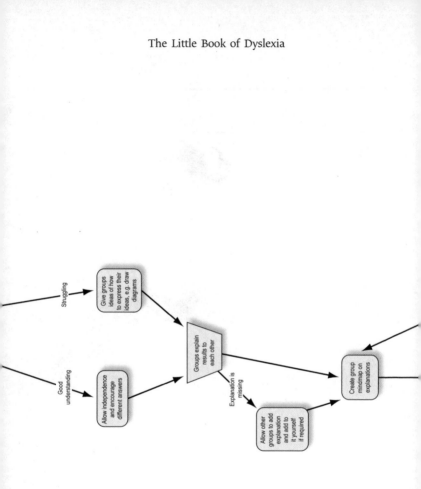

Struggling

Give groups ideas of how to express their ideas, e.g. draw diagrams

Good understanding

Allow independence and encourage different answers

Groups explain results to each other

Explanation is missing

Allow other groups to add explanation and add to it yourself if required

Create group mindmap on explanations

Appendix

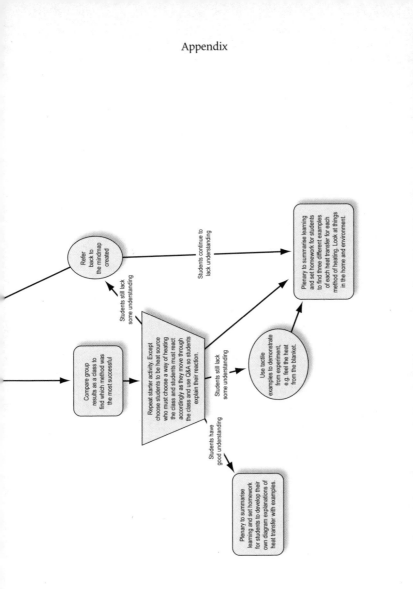

135

Endnotes

Foreword

* A. Reiter, O. Tucha and K. W. Lange, Executive functions in children with dyslexia, *Dyslexia* II, 2005: 116-131. doi: 10.1002/dys.289

** R. Davis, *The Gift of Dyslexia*, Souvenir Press, 2006.

Chapter 1: Introduction

1. J. Jones, *The Magic-Weaving Business: Finding the Heart of Learning and Teaching*. London: Leannta Publishing, 2009.

Chapter 2: Dys-lex-ia

2. See http://www.bdadyslexia.org.uk/about-dyslexia/adults-and-business/dyslexia-and-specific-learning-difficulties-in-adu.html/.

3. L. K. Silverman and J. N. Freed, *The Visual Spatial Learner*. The Dyslexic Reader, 1991. Available at: http://www.dyslexia.com/library/silver1.htm (accessed 5 November 2012).

4. K. Kopko, *Dyslexia and the Brain: Research Shows that Reading Ability Can be Improved*. Cornell University: Human Development Outreach & Extension (n.d.). Available at: http://www.human.cornell.edu/hd/outreach-extension/upload/temple.pdf (accessed 5 November 2012).

5. R. D. Davis, and E. M. Braun. *The Gift of Dyslexia: Why Some of the Smartest People Can't Read ... and How They Can Learn*, rev. edn. Berkeley, CA: Perigree, 2010.

6. J. Gayan and R. K. Olson. Genetic and Environmental Influences on Orthographic and Phonological Skills in Children with reading difficulties. *Developmental Neuropsychology*, 2001, 20(2), 483–507.

7. A. Smith. *The Brain's Behind it: New Knowledge About the Brain and Learning*. Stafford: Network Educational Press, 2002.

8. J. Stein. The magnocellular theory of developmental dyslexia. *Dyslexia* 7, 12–36, 2001. Available at: http://integrativehealthconnection.com/wp-content/uploads/2011/11/The-Magnocellular-Theory-of-Developmental-Dyslexia.pdf (accessed November 5, 2012).

9. M. Young-Scholten and N. Strom. 'First-time adult L2 readers: Is there a critical period?' in I. van de Craats, J. Kurvers, and M. Young-Scholten (eds) *Low-educated adult second language and literacy acquisition* pp. 45–68. Utrecht: LOT, 2006.

10. J. Stein and Z. Kapoula, *Visual Aspects of Dyslexia*. Oxford: Oxford University Press, 2012.

11. P. Ott. *How to Detect and Manage Dyslexia*. A Reference and Resource Manual. Oxford: Heinemann Educational Publishers, 1997.

12. D. J. Johnson and H. R. Myklebust. *Learning Disabilities: Educational Principles and Practices*. New York: Grune and Stratton, 1967.

13. E. Boder. 'Developmental dyslexia: prevailing diagnostic concepts', in H. R. Myklebust (ed.), *Progress in Learning Disabilities and a New Diagnostic Approach*. New York: Grune and Stratton, 1971, pp. 293–321.

14. See J. Rose, *Identifying and Teaching Children and Young People with Dyslexia and Literacy Difficulties. An Independent Report from Jim Rose to the Secretary of State for Children, Schools and Families* [Rose Report]. Nottingham: DCSF, 2009. Available at: https://www.education.gov.uk/publications/eOrderingDownload/00659-

2009DOM-EN.pdf (accessed 26 November 2012); A. Smith, *The Brain's Behind it: New Knowledge about the Brain and Learning,* Stafford: Network Educational Press, 2002; M. Snowling, *Mental Capital and Wellbeing: Making the Most of Ourselves in the 21st Century. State-of-Science Review: SR-D2 – Dyslexia.* London: Government Office for Science/Foresight, 2008. Available at: http://www.bis.gov.uk/foresight/MediaList/foresight/media%20 library/BISPartners/Foresight/docs/mental-capital/~/media/ BISPartners/Foresight/docs/mental-capital/SR-D2_MCW.ashx (accessed 5 November 2012); B. F. Pennington and R. K. Olson, 'Genetics of dyslexia', in M. Snowling and C. Hulme (eds), *The Science of Reading: A Handbook.* Oxford: Blackwell, 2005, pp. 453–472; and J. Stein, The magnocellular theory of developmental dyslexia. *Dyslexia* 7, 2001, 12–36. Available at: http://integrativehealthconnection.com/wp-content/ uploads/2011/11/The-Magnocellular-Theory-of-Developmental-Dyslexia.pdf (accessed 5 November 2012).

15. See A. J. Richardson and M. A. Ross, Fatty acid metabolism in neurodevelopmental disorder: a new perspective on associations between attention-deficit/hyperactivity disorder, dyslexia, dyspraxia and the autistic spectrum. *Prostaglandins, Leukotrienes and Essential Fatty Acids,* 2000, 63(1–2), 1–9; and S. Jeffries and J. Everatt, Working memory: its role in dyslexia and other specific learning difficulties. *Dyslexia,* 2004, 10(3), 196–214.

16. B. F. Pennington. *Diagnosing Learning Disorders,* Guilford; Taylor & Francis, 1991.

17. N. Badian, Reading disability in an epidemiological context: incidence and environmental correlates. *Journal of Learning Disabilities,* 1994, 17(3), 129–136.

18. C. Zabell and J. Everatt, Surface and phonological subtypes of adult developmental dyslexia. *Dyslexia* 8, 2002, 160–177.

19. J. Flynn, The big IQ question. *New Scientist,* 2012, 215(2881), 26–27.

20. J. Flynn, *Asian Americans: Achievement beyond IQ.* Hillsdale, NJ: Erlbaum, 1991.

Chapter 3: The Early Years

21. National Health Service (n.d.). Diagnosing dyslexia. Available at: http://www.nhs.uk/Conditions/Dyslexia/Pages/Diagnosis.aspx (accessed 4 November 2012).

22. A. J. Richardson, and M. A. Ross.Fatty acid metabolism in neurodevelopmental disorder: a new perspective on associations between attention-deficit/hyperactivity disorder, dyslexia, dyspraxia and the autistic spectrum. *Prostaglandins, Leukotrienes & Essential Fatty Acids*, 2000, 63 (1-2), 1–9.

23. See http://www.bdadyslexia.org.uk/about-dyslexia/schools-colleges-and-universities/pre-school-hints.html (accessed 26 November 2012).

24. Department for Education, *Framework for the Early Years Foundation Stage: Setting the Standards for Learning, Development and Care for Children from Birth to Five.* Runcorn: DfE, 2012. Available at: http://media.education.gov.uk/assets/files/pdf/e/eyfs%20statutory%20framework%20march%202012.pdf (accessed 26 November 2012).

Chapter 4: Primary School

25. See http://studentstepstosuccess.com/index.php?sec=intro&sub=main

26. L. Feinstein, Inequality in the early years cognitive development of British children in the 1970 cohort. *Economica*, 2003, 70(277), 73–97.

27. D. Shenk. The 32-Million Word Gap. The Atlantic. Available at: http://www.theatlantic.com/technology/archive/2010/03/the-32-million-word-gap/36856/, 2010, (accessed 5 November 2012).

28. L. Kohlberg, *Essays on Moral Development*, Vol. I: *The Philosophy of Moral Development*. San Francisco, CA: Harper & Row, 1981.

29. B. Wallace, Thinking in context. *Creative Teaching & Learning* 1(4) (n.d.). Available at: www.teachingtimes.com/articles/ctl-1-4_thinking-context.htm (accessed 26 November 2012).

30. L. Sheppard and R. Thorburn-Shears, The design and justification of toolkits to assist people with dyslexia. *The Potass Bulletin*, Winter 2011, 26–30.

Chapter 5: Secondary School

31. See A. Smith, *The Brain's Behind it: New Knowledge about the Brain and Learning*. Stafford: Network Educational Press, 2002.

32. J. Steenhuysen, Optimists live longer and healthier lives: study, 5 March 2009. Available at: http://www.reuters.com/article/2009/03/05/us-optimist-health-idUSTRE5247NO20090305 (accessed 5 November 2012).

33. Pacific Institute, *Investment in Excellence. Personal Resource Manual: From Potential to Performance*. Seattle, WA: Pacific Institute, 2012.

34. C. Dweck, *Mindset: The New Psychology of Success*. New York: Random House, 2007.

Chapter 6: Technology

35. See P. Beadle, *Dancing about Architecture: A Little Book of Creativity*. Carmarthen: Crown House Publishing; and J. W. Young, *A Technique for Producing Ideas*. New York: McGraw-Hill, 2003 [1939].

36. R. Chin, Uncork your brain with mind maps, 15 March 2012. Available at: http://www.innovationexcellence.com/blog/2012/03/15/uncork-your-brain-with-mind-maps (accessed 5 November 2012).

Chapter 7: Exams and Qualifications

37. Department for Education and Skills, *A Framework for Understanding Dyslexia. Delivering Skills for Life: The National Strategy for Improving Adult Literacy and Numeracy Skills*. London: DfES, 2004. Available at: http://www.texthelp.com/media/39354/USAdultLiteracy.pdf (accessed 4 November 2012), 28.

38. A. Smith. *The Brain's Behind it: New knowledge about the brain and learning*. Stafford: Network Educational Press, 2002.

39. C. Kirschbaum, O. T. Wolf, M. May, W. Wippich, D. H. Hellhammer. Stress- and Treatment-Induced Elevations of Cortisol Levels Associated with Impaired Declarative Memory in healthy Adults. *Life Sciences*, 1996, vol.58, 1475–1483.

40. M. Shwartz, Robert Sapolsky discusses physiological effects of stress. Available at: http://news.stanford.edu/news/2007/march7/sapolskysr-030707.html, 7 March 2007, (accessed 5 November 2012).

Chapter 8: Higher Education

41. The forms are available at https://www.gov.uk/disabled-students-allowances-dsas/

42. N. Vidyarthi, Attention spans have dropped from 12 minutes to 5 minutes: how social media is ruining our minds. Available at: http://socialtimes.com/attention-spans-have-dropped-from-12-minutes-to-5-seconds-how-social-media-is-ruining-our-minds-infographic_b86479, 14 December 2011, (accessed 5 November 2012).

Chapter 9: Teaching

43. See http://www.bdadyslexia.org.uk/files/Adult%20Checklist.pdf/

Bibliography

Alexander-Passe, N. (2007). The sources and manifestations of stress amongst school-aged dyslexics, compared with sibling controls. *Dyslexia* 12(4), 291–313.

AQA (2012). Spelling, punctuation and grammar. Available at http://web.aqa.org.uk/support/changes-to-GCSEs/spag.php (accessed 4 November 2012).

Badian, N. (1984). Reading disability in an epidemiological context: incidence and environmental correlates. *Journal of Learning Disabilities* 17(3), 129–136.

Beadle, P. (2011). *Dancing about Architecture: A Little Book of Creativity*. Carmarthen: Crown House Publishing.

Bell, S. (2002). Dyslexia and stress. Available at: http://www.hi2u.org/Dyslexic/dyslexia_and_stress.htm#Dyslexia and stress (accessed 5 November 2012).

Boder, E. (1971). 'Developmental dyslexia: prevailing diagnostic concepts', in H. R. Myklebust (ed.), *Progress in Learning Disabilities and a New Diagnostic Approach*. New York: Grune and Stratton, pp. 293–321.

British Dyslexia Association (n.d.). Dyslexia research information. Available at: http://www.bdadyslexia.org.uk/about-dyslexia/further-information/dyslexia-research-information-.html (accessed 5 November 2012).

Chin, R. (2012). Uncork your brain with mind maps (15 March). Available at: http://www.innovationexcellence.com/blog/2012/03/15/uncork-your-brain-with-mind-maps/ (accessed 5 November 2012).

Chinn, S. (2010). *Addressing the Unproductive Classroom Behaviours of Students with Special Needs*. London: Jessica Kingsley.

Cowley, S. (2010). *Getting the Buggers to Behave*. London: Continuum.

Davis, R. D. and Braun, E. M. (2010). *The Gift of Dyslexia: Why Some of the Smartest People Can't Read … and How They Can Learn*, rev. edn. Berkeley, CA: Perigree.

Department for Education (2012). *Framework for the Early Years Foundation Stage: Setting the Standards for Learning, Development and Care for Children from Birth to Five*. Runcorn: DfE. Available at: http://media.education.gov.uk/assets/files/pdf/e/eyfs%20statutory%20framework%20march%202012.pdf (accessed 26 November 2012).

Department for Education and Skills (2004). *A Framework for Understanding Dyslexia. Delivering Skills for Life: The National Strategy for Improving Adult Literacy and Numeracy Skills*. London: DfES. Available at: http://www.texthelp.com/

media/39354/USAdultLiteracy.pdf (accessed 4 November 2012).

Dweck, C. (2007). *Mindset: The New Psychology of Success*. New York: Random House.

Dyslexia Action (2012). Child assessment. Available at: http://www.dyslexiaaction.org.uk/Pages/FAQs/Default. aspx?Title=child-assessment&IDCategory=a598bb1a-7791-4d44-96c8-5466a5d2e83a&IDTag= (accessed 4 November 2012).

Dyslexia the Gift (2012). Positive aspects of dyslexia. Available at: http://www.dyslexia.com/qagift.htm (accessed 5 November 5 2012).

Eide, B. and Eide, F. (n.d.). Dyslexia and giftedness: how dyslexia presents, and often evades detection, in some of our brightest students. Available at: http://www.scribd.com/ doc/25556209/Dyslexia-and-Giftedness (accessed 5 November 2012).

Everatt, J. and Zabell, C. (2000). 'Gender differences in dyslexia', in I. Smythe (ed.), *The Dyslexia Handbook*. Reading: British Dyslexia Association.

Everatt, J. and Zabell, C. (2002). Surface and phonological subtypes of adult developmental dyslexia. *Dyslexia* 8(3), 160–177.

Farris, A. (2004). *The Other Side of Dyslexia*. San Francisco, CA: Dyslexia Discovery.

Feinstein, L. (2003a). Inequality in the early years cognitive development of British children in the 1970 cohort. *Economica* 70(277), 73–97.

Feinstein, L. (2003b) Very early: how early can we predict future educational achievement? *CentrePiece* (Summer), 24–30. Available at: http://cep.lse.ac.uk/centrepiece/v08i2/feinstein. pdf (accessed 5 November 2012).

Flynn, J. (1991). *Asian Americans: Achievement beyond IQ.* Hillsdale, NJ: Erlbaum.

Flynn, J. (2012). The big IQ question. *New Scientist* 215(2881), 26–27.

Gayan, J. and Olson, R. K. (2001). Genetic and environmental influences on orthographic and phonological skills in children with reading difficulties. *Developmental Neuropsychology* 20(2), 483–507.

Gilbert, I. (2011). *Why Do I Need a Teacher When I've Got Google?* Abingdon: Routledge.

Greed, S. (1994). *Principles of Biopsychology.* Hove: Lawrence Erlbaum Associates.

Jeffries, S. and Everatt, J. (2004). Working memory: its role in dyslexia and other specific learning difficulties. *Dyslexia* 10(3), 196–214.

Bibliography

Johnson, D. and Myklebust, H. (1967). *Learning Disabilities: Education Principles and Practices*. New York: Grune and Stratton.

Jones, J. (2009). *The Magic-Weaving Business: Finding the Heart of Learning and Teaching*. London: Leannta Publishing.

Kirschbaum, C., Wolf, O. T., May, M., Wippich, W., Hellhammer, D.H. (1996) Stress- and Treatment-Induced Elevations of Cortisol Levels Associated with Impaired Declarative Memory in healthy Adults. *Life Sciences* vol.58, 1475–1483.

Kohlberg, L. (1981). *Essays on Moral Development*, Vol. I: *The Philosophy of Moral Development*. San Francisco, CA: Harper & Row.

Kopko, K. (n.d.). Dyslexia and the brain: research shows that reading ability can be improved. Available at: http://www.human.cornell.edu/hd/outreach-extension/upload/temple.pdf (accessed 5 November 2012).

Miles, T. R. (2004). *Dyslexia and Stress*. London: Whurr.

MindTools (n.d.). Are you a positive or negative thinker? Available at: http://www.mindtools.com/pages/article/newTCS_89.htm (accessed 5 November 2012).

MindTools (n.d.). Stress and perception: thinking stress away. Available at: http://www.mindtools.com/stress/rt/IntroPage.htm (accessed 5 November 2012).

National Health Service (n.d.). Diagnosing dyslexia. Available at: http://www.nhs.uk/Conditions/Dyslexia/Pages/Diagnosis.aspx (accessed 4 November 2012).

Newman, D. (2011). Adaptive software: the key for struggling adolescent readers? *Dyslexia Contact* 30(3), 22–26.

Ott, P. (1997). *How to Detect and Manage Dyslexia. A Reference and Resource Manual*. Oxford: Heinemann Educational Publishers.

Pacific Institute (2012). *Investment in Excellence. Personal Resource Manual: From Potential to Performance*. Seattle, WA: Pacific Institute.

Pask, R. and Joy, B. (2007). *Mentoring and Coaching: A Guide for Education Professionals*. Maidenhead: McGraw-Hill Education.

Pennington B. F. (1991). *Diagnosing Learning Disorders*, Guilford; Taylor & Francis.

Pennington, B. F. and Olson, R. K. (2005). 'Genetics of dyslexia', in M. Snowling and C. Hulme (eds), *The Science of Reading: A Handbook*. Oxford: Blackwell, pp. 453–472.

Richardson, A. J. and Ross, M. A. (2000). Fatty acid metabolism in neurodevelopmental disorder: a new perspective on associations between attention-deficit/hyperactivity disorder, dyslexia, dyspraxia and the autistic spectrum. *Prostaglandins, Leukotrienes and Essential Fatty Acids* 63(1–2), 1–9.

Rose, J. (2009). *Identifying and Teaching Children and Young People with Dyslexia and Literacy Difficulties. An Independent Report from Jim Rose to the Secretary of State for Children, Schools and Families* [Rose Report]. Nottingham: DCSF. Available at: https://www.education.gov.uk/publications/eOrderingDownload/00659-2009DOM-EN.pdf (accessed 26 November 2012).

Shenk, D. (2010). The 32-million word gap. Available at: http://www.theatlantic.com/technology/archive/2010/03/the-32-million-word-gap/36856/ (accessed 5 November 2012).

Sheppard, L. and Thorburn-Shears, R. (2011). The design and justification of toolkits to assist people with dyslexia. *The Potass Bulletin* (Winter), 26–30.

Shwartz, M., Robert Sapolsky discusses physiological effects of stress (7 March 2007). Available at: http://news.stanford.edu/news/2007/march7/sapolskysr-030707.html (accessed 5 November 2012).

Silverman, L. K. and Freed, J. N. (1996). The visual spatial learner. *The Dyslexic Reader* 4 (Winter). Available at: http://www.dyslexia.com/library/silver1.htm (accessed 5 November 2012).

Smith, A. (2002). *The Brain's Behind It: New Knowledge about the Brain and Learning*. Stafford: Network Educational Press.

Snowling, M. J. (2008). *Mental Capital and Wellbeing: Making the Most of Ourselves in the 21st Century. State-of-Science Review: SR-D2 – Dyslexia*. London: Government Office for Science/

Foresight. Available at: http://www.bis.gov.uk/foresight/ MediaList/foresight/media%20library/BISPartners/Foresight/ docs/mental-capital/~/media/BISPartners/Foresight/docs/ mental-capital/SR-D2_MCW.ashx (accessed 5 November 2012).

Steenhuysen, J. (2009). Optimists live longer and healthier lives: study (5 March). Available at: http://www.reuters.com/ article/2009/03/05/us-optimist-health-idUS-TRE5247NO20090305 (accessed 5 November 2012).

Stein, J. (2001). The magnocellular theory of developmental dyslexia. *Dyslexia* 7, 12–36. Available at: http://integrative-healthconnection.com/wp-content/uploads/2011/11/ The-Magnocellular-Theory-of-Developmental-Dyslexia.pdf (accessed 5 November 2012).

Stein, J. and Kapoula, Z. (2012). *Visual Aspects of Dyslexia*. Oxford: Oxford University Press.

Shwartz, M. (2007). Robert Sapolsky discusses physiological effects of stress (7 March). Available at: http://news.stanford. edu/news/2007/march7/sapolskysr-030707.html (accessed 5 November 2012).

Times Educational Supplement (TES) (2012). Early learning goals. Available at: http://www.tes.co.uk/teaching-resource/ Early-Learning-Goals-3007398/ (accessed 5 November 2012).

Tree, A. (2008). A brain apart: rethinking our approach to younger learners. *InTuition*, Winter 2008.

Vidyarthi, N. (2011). Attention spans have dropped from 12 minutes to 5 minutes: how social media is ruining our minds (14 December). Available at: http://socialtimes.com/attention-spans-have-dropped-from-12-minutes-to-5-seconds-how-social-media-is-ruining-our-minds-infographic_b86479 (accessed 5 November 2012).

Wallace, B. (n.d.). Thinking in context. *Creative Teaching & Learning* 1(4). Available at: www.teachingtimes.com/articles/ctl-1-4_thinking-context.htm (accessed 26 November 2012).

Young, J. W. (2003 [1939]). *A Technique for Producing Ideas.* New York: McGraw-Hill.

Young-Scholten, M. and Strom, N. (2006). First-time adult L2 readers: Is there a critical period? in I. van de Craats, J. Kurvers, and M. Young-Scholten (Eds.) Low-educated adult second language and literacy acquisition (pp. 45–68). Utrecht: LOT.

Zabell, C. and Everatt, J. (2002). Surface and phonological subtypes of adult developmental dyslexia. *Dyslexia* 8, 160–177.

978-178135089-8

978-178135102-4

978-178135104-8

 www.independentthinkingpress.com